Love Yourself First

Love Yourself First

Letters of Self-Love, Healing and Growth

**Marissa F. Cohen
and 20 Strong, Inspiring Survivors
and Leaders**

Love Yourself First
Letters of Self-Love, Healing and Growth
Publisher: Marissa F. Cohen
www.PublishWithMarissa.com
Cover Art: Photo by Michael Fenton on Unsplash
Cover By: Angie – pro_ebookcovers on Fiverr.com
Publication Date: August 25, 2022
©2023 by Marissa F. Cohen - All Rights Reserved
Printed in USA
ISBN: 9798847401074

ALL RIGHTS RESERVED.

No part of this book or its associated ancillary materials may be reproduced or transmitted in any form by any means including, but not limited to electronic, mechanical, or information storage and retrieval systems – except in the case of brief quotations embodied in critical reviews and articles – photocopying, or recording without the written permission of the author.

DISCLAIMER AND/OR LEGAL NOTICES

While all attempts have been made to verify information provided in this book and its ancillary materials, neither the author or publisher assumes any responsibility for errors, inaccuracies or omissions and is not responsible for any financial loss by customer in any manner. Any slights of people or organizations are unintentional. If advice concerning legal, financial, accounting or related matters is needed, the services of a qualified professional should be sought. This book and its associated ancillary materials, including verbal and written training, is not intended for use as a source of legal, financial or accounting advice. You should be aware of the various laws governing business transactions or other business practices in your particular geographical location.

EARNINGS & INCOME DISCLAIMER

With respect to the reliability, accuracy, timeliness, usefulness, adequacy, completeness, and\or suitability of information provided in this book, Marissa F. Cohen, Marissa F. Cohen, LLC, its partners and associates, affiliates, consultants, and\or presenters make no work warranties, guarantees, representations, or claims of any kind. Readers results will vary depending on a number of factors. Any and all claims or representations as to income earnings are not to be considered as average earnings. Testimonials are not representative. This book and all products and services are for educational and informational purposes only. Use caution and see the advice of qualified professionals. Check with your accountant, attorney or professional advisor before acting on this for any information. You agree that Marissa F. Cohen, and/or Marissa F. Cohen, LLC, is not responsible for the success or failure of your personal, business, health or financial decisions relating to any information presented by Marissa F. Cohen, Marissa F. Cohen, LLC, or company products/services. Earnings potential is entirely dependent on the efforts, skills and application of the individual person.

Any examples, stories, references, or case studies are for illustrative purposes only and should not be interpreted as testimonies and\or examples of what reader and/or consumers can generally expect from the information. No representation in any part of this information, materials, and or seminar trainings are guarantees or promises for actual performance. Any statements, strategies, concepts, techniques, exercises and ideas in the information, materials and\or seminar training offered or simply opinion or experience, and that should not be misinterpreted as promises, typical results or guarantees (expressed or implied). The author and publisher (Marissa F. Cohen, Marissa Cohen LLC, or any of Marissa F. Cohen's representatives) shall in no way, under any circumstances, be held liable to any party (or third-party) for any direct, indirect, punitive, special, incidental or other consequential damages arising directly or indirectly from any use of books, materials and or seminar trainings, which is provided "as is," and without warranties.

This book is based on the real-life personal experience and opinions of the author. Please note that the names and exact places have been changed to protect the identity of those involved. The author will not be held liable or responsible to any person or entity concerning alleged damages caused directly or indirectly by the information within this book.

PRINTED IN THE UNITED STATES OF AMERICA

Love Yourself First
Recognition:

#1 New Release in New Age Mental and Spiritual Healing

#1 Bestseller on Amazon for 1 Consecutive Week

Dedication

This book is dedicated to the people who need to be reminded how incredible they are. Sometimes, we lose our self-love. We start to believe what others say about us, beat ourselves up for being human and making mistakes, and tear ourselves down. This book is a reminder that no matter how dark and down we feel, there's always a light at the end of the tunnel… even when it doesn't seem that way.

You and the 21 authors in this book all have something in common. We've had our darkest days that almost ended it for us. We all experienced pretty awful lows, maybe even hit rock bottom. But there's more in this world for you.

Good things are waiting on the other side of your dark days. Show yourself some love and compassion and you'll get through it.

Dear Reader,

It has been my experience, through the 12+ years of working on my healing, in addition to helping thousands of other survivors find freedom, confidence and peace after trauma, that writing a letter is one of the most effective and impactful way to release the pent-up emotions that you're holding on to. Things you didn't realize are still affecting you may be sitting in the back of your head, your shoulders or your back, causing aches, pains, headaches, and sickness. It's truly amazing (in the worst ways) the way trauma can continue to impact your life. Even when you're not thinking about it, addressing it or paying it any mind. It's there.

One of the first activities I encourage my coaching clients to do is to write themselves a letter. Use this letter to release everything you're holding on to, whether you know it or not. Just write. Show yourself the love and compassion that you deserve. But more importantly, encourage yourself to know that you're not alone, and that you have strength, resilience and people in your corner to help you out of your situation.

This is often met with resistance because it can be uncomfortable. So, if they're stuck, I instruct them to put their best friend in the situation they're facing, or pretend a friend or family member expressed how this survivor is feeling. What would they say to them? What would you say to your best friend if they were experiencing what you're experiencing or have experienced? Chances are you would show them kindness and support. Encourage them to love themselves and see the situation from your perspective. That they are strong, and they're not alone. Right?

Why don't we do that for ourselves? Why don't we show ourselves the same love and compassion that we show our best friends?

Letter writing is a powerful tool that you can use to overcome almost anything. I have personal and private notebooks filled with letters to myself, the people that hurt me, abusers and narcissists, family members and friends after fights, etc. I never give them to the people they're addressed to; this is an exercise just for me (and now for you).

Use this to let go of all the crap you're holding on to, and you'll feel an emotional release. That cloudy, hazy brain will finally clear up, and the stress and physical pain (if you have any) might just go away.

The key here is to be your biggest ally. It's easier said than done, I know. But this is a step along your journey. Know that I'm proud of you, we're all proud of you, and you can overcome your trauma.

Our traumas don't define us, but they guide us in a direction towards our best lives. The climb to the top can be rough, but the view from up there is incredible.

Always remember, regardless of your experiences, you're not alone.

You are Braver than you believe,
Stronger than you seem,
Smarter than you think,
And, Loved more than you know.

Sincerely,

Marissa F. Cohen

Marissa F. Cohen

TABLE OF
CONTENTS

Foreword by Danielle Sammut 2

Foreword by Victoria Andreola 6

Maria's Letter 8

Orsika's Letter 14

Vicki's Letter 18

Tiffany's Letter 22

Danielle's Letter 26

Mara's Letter 34

Alma Jean's Letter 38

Leah's Letter 42

Victoria's Letter 46

TALIA'S LETTER	56
MEGAN RENEE'S LETTER	62
SARAH'S LETTER	66
KIMMIE'S LETTER	72
MELINDA'S LETTER	76
LOGAN'S LETTER	84
WANDA'S LETTER	88
STACEY'S LETTER	94
NANA'S LETTER	98
MAUREEN'S LETTER	106
JULIET'S LETTER	112
MARISSA'S LETTER	118

FOREWORD

By: Danielle Sammut

All of us have been to dark and painful places. Me, you, your neighbor, your childhood teacher, the lady behind you at the grocery store, and even that angry driver who beeped their horn at you too many times. How do we rally the courage, time after time, to believe that there are brighter days ahead and grow through the problems we face? That willpower is the powerful force called self-love, which arms us to overcome life's obstacles and become stronger warriors with each challenge.

Theodor Seuss Geisel, who is famous for writing the children's classic *Oh, The Places You'll Go*, shared a piece of wisdom that has become a guiding quote in my life: "When something bad happens you have three choices. You can either let it define you, let it destroy you, or you can let it strengthen you."

When I was a tender age of ten, my Uncle Stephen died on the 84th floor of The World Trade Center on September 11, 2001. My childhood would never be the same again. Every holiday, as I witnessed the hearts of my family breaking again in his absence, I felt the scars pressing more deeply into my soul. There were days I would lean against the bay window in my living room and stare at the Henry Hudson trail wishing that maybe my uncle was just lost, for a very long time, and that he was finally making his way back to us. To conquer the depression that ensued at only 13-year-old, I poured my heart into writing dark, cathartic poetry in my journal that gave me a safe space to process my feelings.

Within a few short years, I published nearly 60 poems on a poetry blog and began to discover the healing power of words.

As a teenager, I often felt alone because not many kids in my classes could relate to what my family had experienced. Perhaps there was someone just like me, sitting in Language Arts class, fighting back tears, suffering in silence, but stuck inside their own head because they never dared to tell a soul how they really felt. Reading was my outlet and, at times, a critical life line to help me escape and learn how characters my own age have bravely overcome these struggles—no matter the odds, no matter the complications. I found comfort in reading books that made me feel like there were other people, just like me, who were suffering too, in their own unique way. I especially connected with the main characters from realistic fiction books, like Caitlin from *Dreamland* by Sarah Dessen, who felt powerless at first, but eventually found the courage to speak up and seek help.

Every day in my middle school Language Arts classroom, I have the power as an educator to give my students the assurance that they have at least one "happy place" in their day. Our expansive classroom library is filled with thousands of contemporary and classic books with messages about hope, humanity, and endless possibilities that broaden their perspective on the human psyche and strengthen how they relate to the people around them. I have been able to turn my pain into purpose, making a career out of instilling the love of reading into generations of young hearts and pushing them to find their writing voice so that they can express themselves to the world. My students will never feel powerless as I did when I was younger.

In my personal story, which I share with you just beyond this page, I discuss a transformative moment in my life that made me want to expand this healing power to an audience beyond my classroom walls. The moment that reignited my warrior spirit and gave me the wisdom to inspire others to begin their own journeys of self-love, improving their minds, bodies, and spirits as they fight life's hardships and find peace. My mission, and the goal of this book, is to give people the courage to accept that everyone's journey of self-love is different, so they can be free to live their most authentic life.

James Baldwin once said, "You think your pain and your heartbreak is unprecedented in the history of the world, but then you read. It was books that taught me that the things that tormented me most were the very things that connected me with all the people who were alive, who had ever been alive." In this collection, you will hear from brave authors who share personal stories from their past and explore how they have been shaped and strengthened by their most horrific moments. These heart-wrenching and gripping retellings may shock audiences, but ultimately serve as safe spaces for these individuals, from all walks of life, to heal and grow. They won't let their bad situations define them or destroy them because their lives can now serve to inspire other people, who may be living in their own dark places, that there will always be salvation and brighter days ahead, no matter how distant that light may seem.

FOREWORD

By: Victoria Andreola

The textbook definition of a warrior is, "A person who fights in battles and is known for having courage and skill. A person engaged in some struggle or conflict."

If you're reading this book, then chances are you are in fact a warrior, or are in need of a little motivation from people who have overcome what you're experiencing. I know I am. Much like our author, Marissa F. Cohen. The founder of the Healing From Emotional Abuse Philosophy, a survivor, an overcomer, and an example of healing. The power of giving back when one has overcome so many obstacles in life, is exactly the reason why we have outlets today. People like Marissa are what helps those who feel like they're going through this journey alone. With over 24,000 listeners a week on her podcast, 5 published books, and her nonprofit organization, Within Your Reach, Inc., Marissa has exceeded any and all expectations what a warrior truly is.

Life is crazy. Life is also extremely strange. Things happen in life beyond our control. If you are a victim of sexual, physical, emotional, mental abuse, or the various other types of traumas that fall into this category, then I would suggest to keep reading. Abuse comes in many difference forms, with many different faces, as we know, but what matters is how we overcome it.

In the midst of trauma, we convince ourselves that it's what we deserve. When you become so accustomed to being treated a certain way, you believe that's how it is supposed to be. Well, speaking for myself and countless other survivors, we are here to tell you that, that's not the case. It takes time, perseverance, and self-confidence.

When you feel like your back is literally and figuratively up against the wall, you can find yourself questioning how you got there. You may ask yourself, "Why me?" It took me years to understand my true self before I was able to fully heal.

Remember, it's okay to have a bad day. **It will be a bad day, not a bad life**. You're allowed, even after your healing process, to relive and revisit old wounds, as long as you do it in hindsight and not regret.

All the pain we have endured by individuals in our lifetimes, it is time for us to regain our self-worth and remember everybody did what was best for them. It's your turn. Believe you deserve it, and you will have it. We've had enough lessons in life, and have overcome so many different obstacles. We believed when we knew it was hard to. We pushed through it all to get to this point of self-sacrifice and a chance at getting what we deserve.

Dear 2006 Me,

I'm going to tell you all of the great things in your life first. I'm so proud of you for getting so far. You're married to a wonderful, loving man and you're expecting your first child. You got your degree after years of hard work and being told you weren't good enough. You found yourself at a job where you're valued… but you went through hell and back to get there. Thank God you never gave up and figured out who was truly there for you.

You didn't know it, but in 2006 when you moved in with that handsome, older man, he was grooming you. He manipulated you to think he cared, but he took advantage of a poor relationship with your father and exploited your feelings. He welcomed you into his family, moved you into his house, then criticized you any chance he got. He would love bomb you and insist on frequent intimacy, knowing it would make you more attached. One day you woke up, though. One day, you decided you had enough of living the way you were and your amazing mother came and packed your things and brought you home.

Coming home didn't mean the relationship with dad would all of a sudden be perfect. You insisted this move was temporary until you could get out on your own. You did achieve that, but the emotional cost would prove to be too high after several years. You had your apartment and you met some new guy at work that was going through a terrible breakup, at least according to him. He was suddenly left after years, cheated on, and broken. You recently had heartbreak, so you decided you could lean on each other. Little did you know, this too was a manipulation tactic.

At one point, you decided to get Brody. He was truly a life saver and reminder of unconditional love. However, this was now the "in" that those who shall not be named (he doesn't deserve that dignity) needed to slide into living with you without so much as a conversation other than, "I guess you'll need me to move in and help with the dog." It sounded like a sincere thought at the time, then turned into freeloading. By that time though, you were in love and just didn't realize. You got engaged and started planning your wedding, only to find out you were cheated on. You were both living at mom and dads to save money, so it was easy to get him out and not disrupt your daily life. But he wouldn't let you move on. He tracked your phone, he drove by the house, all in the name of "love." At some point, you broke down and took him back. He proposed again, you accepted, but this time you went through with the wedding. It's funny. The night before, your friend offered you an escape plan. You brushed off the raging anxiety and insisted it was just cold feet and that everything would be ok. I sure wished you listened.

Not too long after finally moving into your new home together, the switch flipped. You couldn't do anything on your own. You couldn't have a moment of peace - not in the bathroom or even the shower. According to him, if you wanted to be alone in those moments it meant you were sending out nude pictures. You couldn't go grocery shopping alone either. God Forbid you tried to go out with a girlfriend. You were followed and interrogated. That wouldn't be the worst of it though. After being broken down psychologically for months and not having the desire to have sex, he decided it was time to force you. He forced himself on you, forced your clothes off, and made sure his need was met. He's so callous and so psychotic, he thought nothing of saying, "It feels like I just raped you." You looked at him dead in the face and said, "Because you did." You cried and cried and punished yourself to the couch from there on out. Your brother's wedding was coming up and there was no way you wanted to cause any emotional pain to your family before such a joyous event, so you stuck it out. Again, he love-bombed to try and get you to just forgive him.

The night of the wedding, after all of the partying was done, you knew you were done too - especially after his mother came up to you to ask you what you've done to her son in the middle of the reception. You knew this was no longer between the two of you. The mission for him was to be the victim and to make you the villain. You went back to your hotel room and you fought and screamed. He trapped you in that room and held you against the door as you struggled to get out from his hold. You hoped anyone would hear you and call the police. You prayed and prayed, but no one came. When all was finally calm, and the psychotic episode was over, the cycle began again. Instead of fighting, you tried a different tactic to avoid it starting again. You leaned into the "kindness" and made him believe that you believed him. This was your survival tactic.

On your way home, he made sure to stop and buy you something nice. Another classic narcissist move. But your plan was in place. You took a half day from work that following Friday, let your family know, and let Marissa know. No questions asked, Marissa came at the perfect time, helped you pack your clothes, and got you out of there without an explanation to him or anyone in his family. You took Brody and your things and everything else was left behind. It didn't matter. You didn't know how strong you were at the time or even how you mustered up the courage, but you know now. You were freed. You saved yourself from a lifetime of abuse.

In those days, there were so many emotions. You were scared, anxious, confused how you didn't see all the red flags. Now, you can say you feel nothing but pride. You defeated those odds, you've worked on yourself, and you've come out of everything with a more beautiful life than you can imagine. You're a survivor. You will forever celebrate October 9th as your personal Independence Day. You're going to do more though.

You're going to teach your children the signs. You'll teach them what true love is. You'll hope they remember your words and your actions. When they're old enough, you'll tell them the story of how you met their father and everything that led you to him. You'll work diligently to hopefully help at least one person out of a terrible situation so they can be free too.

"She was unstoppable, not because she did not fail or have doubts, but she continued on despite them."

Love,

2022 Maria

About the Author

Maria opted to be anonymous, but we thought we should brag for her. Maria is a strong, courageous, fierce survivor who has climbed mountains to get to where she is now. We are so beyond proud of the person she has grown into through her self-work and self-care. We love you so much for sharing your story. Thank you for empowering survivors through your willingness to share your story, and your journey.

Oh, Sweet Girl,

This season in life simply sucks. It is the darkest time you've ever experienced. You feel lost, depressed (though you don't admit it), and alone. You want to crawl into a small space, cry, and never come back up. You want to drink every night to numb yourself from the realities. How did you get here? How did you allow yourself to be in a relationship that is fake, volatile, and demeaning?

Do the 'how's' matter at this point? In reality, no. What matters are the glimpses of hope holding onto you. Those glimpses of hope come in the form of three outstanding blessings who have been bestowed upon you. Those glimpses of hope keep you going every single day. As you suffer in silence and feel as though the world is collapsing around you, those three glimpses of hope need you today just as much as when they're 22, 20, and 14.

Yes, baby girl, you'll all get there. A decade from now, they will come to you in confidence, in the good times and the challenges, in the laughter and the tears. They will respect you on a level you don't even think possible because you struggle with self-respect in the lifeless void of today.

I'll be honest with you, before you get there, before you reach the ten-year mark of freedom, you'll lose things most precious to you - Apa, Granddaddy, Turbo, TJ, friends and lovers. But you'll know how to handle the loss, and you'll come through stronger than ever. Your strength building begins today. Today, you will stand up for yourself for the first time; you will start believing in yourself again. Today, you begin the journey of self-love.

Interestingly enough, you're learning to love yourself for your children. You know they learn from your actions more than your words. You are fully aware they watch your movements, your reactions, your heart. They see you crying deep inside. They see you struggling. They see your pain. You want better for *them.* Therefore, you push through the pain of having been raped by your spouse. You push through the pain of emotional, psychological, and spiritual abuse. You push through the pain of living in survival mode with PTSD for the next five years.

Slowly, during the half decade, you'll grow out of the darkness. You'll see your little angels continually inspire you to become the best version of yourself. You will begin trusting your heart again. You'll allow yourself to be vulnerable and inspiring. Oh, sweet girl, the things you will accomplish are remarkable.

Your journey is filled with self-discovery, self-acceptance, and self-love. You will learn to look inward for all three. Your happiness and contentment will come from within. Your faith journey will be like no other, as you recognize a million little miracles each day. Your light will shine more and more brilliantly with a decade's worth of trips around the sun. You learn to be still without fear. You dream without nightmares. You walk with confidence. Laughter and peace replace the seemingly endless tears. You begin to journal, practice yoga, go to the chiropractor, and take long walks with those closest to you. You remember to dance and to write. You take beach days and marvel at the calm of crisp Michigan winters. These are your raindrops on roses and whiskers on kittens. These are a few of your favorite things.

Somewhere along the way, you forgive the inequities you've chosen. You forgive yourself and the others who pushed you into the quicksand. Somewhere along the way, you understand the value of personal development. Somewhere along the way, you become a certified trainer with one of the most influential people to walk this planet. Somewhere along the way, you guide others on their own healing journey. Will you have triggers? Yes. Will you overcome them? Absolutely. And, somewhere along the way, you find yourself.

With my entire being, I love you the best I know how,

Me

About the Author

Orsika Julia is a daughter and sibling to Hungarian refugees. She grew up in a suburb of Chicago. As a child, she spent time figure skating, dancing, doing gymnastics, and horseback riding - just to name a few activities.

Orsika's childhood was magical. As an adult, her choices were less than amazing. She moved from one failed relationship to another, had three children, and lost direction in life. She felt as though she let everyone down. Having experienced domestic violence, Orsika knew something had to change. She hit rock bottom and knew in her soul the years of abuse were going to drastically transform her life for the better.

Her healing journey began well after escaping the abuse. Orsika lived through the pain, the shame, and the guilt of making decisions which brought sorrow and potential unforgiveness. She understands, firsthand, the feelings of loneliness and desperation.

Now, on the other side of the mountain, Orsika is a motivational speaker, author, and Certified Canfield Trainer. Along with beach days, her loved ones, and her vast plethora of pets, Orsika enjoys creating programs to guide others on their healing journey so they can live a life of purpose, forgiveness, and peace.

Dear Victoria 2015,

Please wake up. You can't go out like this. In this hospital bed? Not like this. Wake up.

There you are.

Ring a bell?

I know right now you probably feel like there is no hope for you. You want to run away. But please hang in there and don't run anymore. Fear isn't what you've always thought. Fear stands for face everything and recover. Remember?

I know. The years of trauma, abuse, and manipulation has led you to this path of destruction within your addiction. This drug makes you feel loved. They didn't. This drug makes you feel safe. They didn't. Warm? Yeah well, they didn't do that either. But this drug makes you feel sick when you don't have it. Didn't you feel sick when he hit you for no reason? Didn't you feel sick when no one believed you were sexually assaulted, until he was arrested? Isn't this drug doing the same thing, nearly? If you haven't figured it out yet, these toxic relationships were like drugs Victoria. If one came to an end why can't the other. You're human, and easily replaced one for another. The abuse you've endured truly had you believe you weren't good enough for anyone or anything. What about your dreams? Wrestling, a family, children?

Believe me I understand what it's like to feel this way, even now. I can promise you, life isn't going to be easy, but you'll come to see how much better things will truly be. You'll come to find out, you might stumble across another man or two who might show you a different side of abuse like narcissism, and control. But I can tell you - if you embark on this journey of self-discovery and recovery, you will find the tools you never knew you had. You'll be able to navigate the crazy world, and realize you aren't wrong. You'll be able to remember where you never want to end up again. You may even come across a guy who will finally give you the self-respect you deserve. But first, it has to come from you.

I've seen you at your best, and at your absolute worst. You have had every right to feel every ounce of sorrow, pain, regret, remorse, and wondering of, "why me."

But think of our family. If it wasn't for them. I wouldn't be here today. I wouldn't be able to write this to you, and tell you how proud of you I am.

For being driven to your near-death by an abuser in 2008. I have memories of that day as well. Sitting in the car, on the parkway, watching the trees go by, literally believing I was being driven to my death. From telling a 21-year-old to please stop at 15. From losing Uncle Eddie, Grandpa Frank and Grandpa Hank back-to-back in 2007. Once they died, you truly believed aside from your father every man you've ever loved has left you. From court rooms to therapy. Now beating this addiction - you've been through it all, and I still think about these things from time to time. But today, I can share my story and help others find their path to self-discovery. I can see patterns not only in others but in myself because of YOU.

You made it through several storms back then and I still are today. The ride of life is still bumpy, but it's manageable. If you didn't do the work, I wouldn't be alive today. I love you, and I always will.

Remember, "The future belongs to those who believe in the beauty of their dreams."

I know you can't see it yet, but you'll come to find out how many people you will have touched in so many ways emotionally. How many people you will help. How many people will look up to you like you looked up to your hero Lita in wrestling. You'll be able to share your story constantly, and you'll be able to connect with more people than you ever imagined. You will live your dream, because I am living it now. I think with our personality, we will always have fear of the unknown. And from you being so fearless, I've become a little fearful as I got older. But the one thing that stands as I get through everything, you will find your family friends and loved ones constantly telling you how strong you are and how much they admire you. You will be able to stand in front of a crowd of people and tell them your abuse story. Tell them your addiction story. And with your wrestling, you will have a large platform to do that. I know you felt like dying more than once, and I know you had no self-respect. But now you do, and I thank you for that every single day.

That's a quote I got from you and I'll never forget it.

Thanks for believing in yourself because now I believe in me.

Love you endlessly.

Victoria 2022

About the Author

Victoria Andreola is a professional wrestler who goes by the ring name "Vicious Vicki. "Professionally wrestling for over 5 years, Victoria has always found her fan-following through wrestling as a sound foundation to share her story to inspire others.

She has created her own recovery resource online center called 'Dying To Live,' and personal training business 'Vicious Hustle Fitness.'

A woman who wears many hats, she is always expanding and exploring all different avenues.

Dear Tiffy,

As a child, you endured so much abuse in so many different forms, and you carried that with you from childhood into adulthood. You accepted less than what you deserved or desired. Tiffy, you loved and always saw the best in people, and the best in the worst situations. You always had hope, even when you felt life was hopeless.

Your exes would always try to control you; Make you feel less than. Narcissistic abuse, psychological and physical abuse. You were sexualized when you were young and didn't know what real love was. Even though you were hurt so many times, you always tried to see the good in people. You always tried to fix them, love them and help them... only to hurt yourself. Years went by and you continued to endure so much pain, so much sadness in relationships and other areas in your life.

But, I m so proud of who you have become. You re a strong, independent, lover-of-all, capable woman. I love how you always see the good and also can sense danger. We call this, 'hyper-vigilance.' I wish you could drop that, but it has protected you from dangerous situations.

It just takes one moment. One small moment that made me change my mind and leave an abuser. I will never forget the day I was in my ex's room. He had gotten mad at me because I would not do something. He smacked the phone out of my hand after I had been awake for less than ten minutes. My son, who was two at the time, looked so afraid. He looked helpless with his big beautiful eyes staring at me like he wanted to help me but couldn't. As if he had seen a ghost and was frozen. I felt so much sadness and anger in that moment. I knew we needed to leave. I would not let him grow up to see a man treat women that way and think it's okay that he treats a woman the same way. So, we packed up and left.

I'll never forget the woman s shelter we stayed in for three months, terrified to leave just in case he was outside or around the corner. I didn't visit my family for the longest time in fear that he may drive by and see me or my car. Every time I went outside for a cig or to breathe, I was filled with fear and sadness. I hated it... I felt so alone. So afraid for what the future held for the kids and I.

That was just one a** hole you dealt with. There were others after. But that was the moment you started loving yourself and protecting yourself. That was THE MOMENT that you realized there is so much more in this world than just four walls and some guy yelling at you and abusing your babies. I'll never forget the time we went to counseling together, and by the next appointment, he was not with me. The counselor said Oh, thank God you left him! He was horrible and he blamed YOU for being abused in the past." In that moment you knew you were DONE.

My best friend, my life long best friend. She called me all the time. Even though she lived hundreds of miles away. I knew I needed to listen and she would always tell me to leave. I am so glad I did. I really think she saved me.

I started writing music again, singing, cooking, exercising and really giving my all to myself. Then, I watched this show a few years later. I realized I needed to love myself 100% or I d always accept love that was less than that. (Daniel Sloss-Netflix) He said, If you don t love yourself at 100%, you will accept love less than that. You can love yourself at 20% and someone comes in and loves you at 30% and you think OMG this person loves me; but they don t fully love you. Not all of you."

I started to open my eyes and realize that I have a heart of gold. I want to help so many people but I need to do it in the right way. I m smarter than I realized and I m still learning more and more about myself each day.

If you want to know if you are in the right relationship, do this one thing (and this applies to all relationships you have in your life):

Get a photo of you as a child. Go over any arguments or conversations you have had as that person. Repeat those words from the conversations to your child photo. Ask yourself, "Does this kid deserve these words? Did they deserve to be spoken to or yelled at like that?" And if you can honestly say, This is the love that child deserves," then you re in a healthy relationship. If not, you may want to consider leaving the situation. This applies to every relationship: friends, family, your partner, boss, coworkers. It doesn t matter who. You may find yourself ending a lot of relationships that you never realized were toxic, and you may feel grief, I know I did. But no matter how old we get, our inner child is still there, deep inside of us just wanting to love and be loved.

I m so proud of you for learning tricks and tips to get out of bad situations, Tiffy. There is still so much more work to do and things to learn.

I know sometimes you still cry in your room and you hate being alone, I know you re still afraid to open up to someone, but one day it will happen. You ll be ready and you will know when it s safe. You've held your guard up for so long, please let it fall. Please allow love to come to you when it is genuine. Please breathe again. Please let your warrior side take a rest every once in a while, and remember to be more gentle.

Love Always,

Tiffany.

About the Author

Co-Author Tiffany Kramer. Tiffany is planning to release her first published book in 2023, delving into her past trauma and she overcame abuse from childhood through adulthood.

She's a mother of 3, coffee lover, and an abuse and trauma survivor.

Sneak Peek: Learning how to heal, foods that increase happiness and relieve anxiety to become your best self will all be discussed in her upcoming book! Look out for it in 2023!

Dear Danielle,

When you were a little kid, you were told to watch out for the monsters hidden under your bed, but what they didn't warn you about are the monsters all around you. The ones in plain sight are the ones we truly need to be afraid of. There he was, James Dean incarnated, with that captivating grin and irresistible charm. Yet he had trickery up his sleeve like the most wicked villain of fairytales. He carried a poison apple that tasted so sweet like a forbidden fruit. One bite could send you into your wildest dream, but another could very well place you in the glass casket, waiting for the kiss of a prince to bring you back to life. This monster, like a wolf with razor sharp teeth, can turn your fairytale vision into the most twisted tragedy you can no longer bear to experience.

You have been berated and shaken. You have seen texts to his exes. Windshields shattered. Gifts tossed out the window. You have been burned by his slurs. You have cried yourself to sleep. You have sobbed to your friends. You have been silenced, threatened, coerced, controlled. You have lived on egg shells. You have given him a chance to tell the truth. You have given him every part of your heart–even the parts that have been poisoned by his love.

You had never felt more alive. You had never felt a love more thrilling. A euphoria, an ecstasy of the spirit. Like Florida Georgia Line, he made you want to "roll your window down and cruise." He was your Prince Charming, your protection, your hero. He came to your rescue and fiercely claimed you. He encouraged and believed in you. He made you dream of family and home. He made you envision your higher self. He completed you.

Until you realized that there was nothing left of you. You could no longer recognize yourself. Frail bones. Bare pockets. A broken home. You had been wrapped into a fantasy of the potential of this person, rather than seeing him for who he was. Someone incredibly flawed and wounded. Someone that was incapable of being the partner you needed. Yet you felt like a failure to society's expectations and trapped by the opinions of others. You allowed the fear of their judgment to keep you in a relationship that was toxic to your mental health. And so, you tried desperately to salvage something that never really existed.

You scribbled poems in your notebook to dull the throbbing pain. Your heart was breaking a little more each day. Mourning the love that could never be:

> "What is left when the heart breaks?
> A heart that resembles a twisted doll from a nightmare
> Shaped like an overgrown child with a crooked grin
> With lightning bolt stitches stretched across its face
>   with a soulless hollow center
> that reverberates the sound of love songs
> And flashes memories that bite at your core."

Questions from family, friends–even strangers–swarmed you and intensified the pain. The incessant questions about your relationship status and future plans to marry and have children. *I could never get those years back*, I thought. *How can I start over?*

You thought another dose of love would heal your trauma. You were certain that the right person was out there, ready to save you and give you everything your heart desired. Like arrows shot from a bow, shards of the last relationship pierced you again. You continued to accept the things that you swore you never would. Same issues. Different partner.

Flipping your notebook back open, you turned to writing again to express what was stirring inside:

> "Why does it hurt when the heart breaks?
> long after a special hand stitched it back to life?"

The wound was still there because you never gave yourself a chance to be alone and truly process your feelings. You simply did not have time to waste when society told you that you needed to meet the "right" guy by 30, as if a bomb explodes at this age and your life is over...

And then you turned 30. You had the same type of impending doom that we all did on December 31, 1999 when we thought the computers would crash on Y2K. The computers adapted with ease. Could you? No matter the difficulty, you needed a change.

You were single for the first time, unattached, with no prospects of a serious relationship. Then it dawned on you. You had never spent any time investing in a relationship with yourself. The most important relationship you will ever have in your life. Now was the time to make a bold and powerful choice to press pause on the matchmaking and press play on dating yourself.

Being independent gave you wings. Living on your own provided you with the space to lead a healthier lifestyle and to discover the woman that was hidden behind the shadows of others. You joined Orangetheory Fitness and began releasing your stress on the treadmill and challenged yourself by lifting heavy weights. Each time you increased your heart rate, you were shedding the trauma, drip by drip, as you were pouring your energy into your own wellbeing. Over time, the physical changes you could see in the gym translated to a more radiant energy that people could feel.

Then you hired a nutritionist to get you "stage ready" for your first ever beauty pageant. This pageant system was diversified, inclusive, and focused on women being strong leaders in their communities–a role that came with ease, a role you wanted to develop further. Your nutritionist counseled you on how to eat balanced, nutritious meals that were tailored to your goal of building muscle. Finally, you were fueling your body with the proper macronutrients, the right amount of protein, carbohydrates, and fats to help you curb the binge eating habit you had been struggling with your entire life. This lifestyle change required discipline and consistency, which ultimately meant structuring your schedule and creating boundaries that you never had for yourself. Suddenly, you were no longer available on a whim because you had goals to achieve that could not be compromised. You were putting yourself first.

You poured your heart into your classroom. As a 7th grade language arts teacher, you had survived remote learning and were finally able to return to your physical classroom, "a happy place" for you and the students. You spent hours of your personal time buddy reading books like *The Pants Project* and *George* because you could relate to these misunderstood protagonists–people striving to be themselves, unapologetically, without backlash from society. As the kids bustled into the school building each day, you would greet each child with a special good morning wish and would designate time to chat with the students in your book club. Their passion for reading grew exponentially. Your investment in them ignited a passion for reading that would propel them in life. At this time, you started to realize how powerful and precious your energy is, which taught you to evaluate the people in your life to gauge whether they only drain your energy or fuel you to accomplish good.

Your former self, suffocated by heartache, seems distant now. Healing for you was a years-long, arduous process of accepting what was and building safe places for yourself, and within yourself, so that you could become the woman you always knew you were capable of being.

> "The pain is a stain
> And if I could just –
> Remove it –
> I could be a blank slate once again.
>
> Free from the echoes
> Of the raging birds that haunt me
> With their ravenous squawks
> With their piercing claws
> That strike dents in my mind
>
> This bleeding heart melts
> Into my hands
> -Tacky-
> -Cold-
> I toss it away
> And like a boomerang
> It smacks back into me
> And knocks me over once more."

The dark poetry you once scribbled in your notebook in the wee hours of the night transformed into healing messages on social media. You not only wanted to grow through your pain, but you wanted others in your life to feel empowered to go through this same metamorphosis. Your soul was sent on a mission to heal others by sharing your story, even the parts you were too afraid to share. *Be the best version of yourself,* you would say. *Mind, body, and spirit.* The outpouring of energy you once devoted to your partner was now invested in yourself. You made time to read, exercise, eat three meals a day, maintain a skin care routine, and discover your personal style. You researched your birth chart and began to reflect on your patterns, your quirks, your triggers, the things that made you a perfectly imperfect human being, and a partner who deserves all the love in the world despite all her flaws. You made a daily commitment that had many setbacks and challenges, just like relationships with others, but this time, the love that grew in return was a love that could light up the world.

As much as you would have liked to believe that someone, somewhere would save you from the darkness, you discovered that loving yourself was the only true rescue. Instead of swimming around the depths of your despair, hiding from the pain, you realized that growth is not found there. True growth, true self development, truly reaching your highest potential was only possible when you finally stopped waiting. Your journey began when you decided that you would take one step towards the light every day, no matter how small, rather than ever again fall back into the darkness that you fought so hard to escape. Having always deep down had the strength to help yourself, you finally took the leading role in your life, choosing every day to love yourself unapologetically. You have rewritten your story from a grim tale of monsters haunting the princess trapped in her tower and reimagined it as the remarkable quest for a queen, as the hero of her own story, to be the best version of herself. The light from her tower shines so bright that no one, not even herself, can dim this light. For the light that shines within her soul can defeat any monster, even the ones that live within herself.

I truly love you,

Danielle

About the Author

Danielle Sammut has been teaching middle school language arts for the past decade. She prides herself in motivating young people to find their writing voice and develop a life-long passion for reading. She makes her classroom a safe place for her students to take risks and ultimately reach their highest potential.

Danielle's mission in life is to empower youth through the vehicle of reading and community service. As Miss New Jersey for America Strong 2022, she has partnered with The Bridge of Books Foundation to provide underserved children across New Jersey with access to high-interest reading experiences. She enjoys organizing book drives in her local community and creating free Book Ark libraries to help unite community members. As someone who did not have opportunities to travel growing up, she understands the importance of bringing the world to kids through books to broaden their perspectives on life.

She is also a dedicated member of the New Jersey District of Kiwanis, an organization that inspires and nurtures children around the world by mentoring them in service-learning programs. Throughout the past 13 years, she been honored with the organization's most prized honors for her devotion to the youth of New Jersey. In March 2022, she was named Alumni of the Year for her service as an advisor of her school's Builders Club; this Kiwanis-sponsored youth program gives students opportunities to develop their character through service and leadership. Having been a distinguished state and international officer of her Kiwanis youth group growing up, she is proud to mold the next generation of youth just as her mentors empowered her as a teenager. Ultimately, Danielle wants to use her platform to give kids more opportunities to discover their passions, find their voice, and be change-makers in their community.

She currently lives on the Jersey shore and spends her free time working out at Orangetheory Fitness, modeling as a brand ambassador, and trying out new, healthy recipes in her kitchen!

Dear Mara,

This one hurt. No doubt about it. I know you have endured a narcissistic parent, mental/emotional abuse, and a handful of uncomfortable moments with family members and random men, but this one left a void that seemed impossible to fill.

At the time, it was easier to forget the event all together for 5 years. You had almost completely locked it out of your brain. You felt great. Like nothing had ever happened. You traveled, you loved, you moved across the country. You accomplished great things during your time of denial. Those accomplishments gave you strength. Even if you didn't realize it at the time.

It wasn't until you were faced with another similar moment of terror that your memories came flooding back. In a matter of seconds, you were transported back in time, reliving the pain you once hid from yourself for many years. The touch, the fear, your voice falling on deaf ears and your reaction to then freeze, close your eyes and just pray for it to end. The worst part being the period of shame that followed; a feeling so intense, it felt as real as the blood that dripped down your legs.

But, this time wasn't like the last time. This time you spoke up louder. This time you *pushed*, you forcefully said no until your voice was so loud that man had no choice but to hear. My love, you made sure your voice was heard. No, this time wasn't going to be like last time. There would be no penetration, no guilt, no shame, and no blood (unless it was theirs). This time, there would be strength, hope, survival, and pride.

Even though you came out physically unscathed, the months to follow were emotionally hard. You could no longer ignore what happened 5 years ago. It was here, front and center, to stay. Your choice was to let it devour you and control your every thought, or for you to rise to power. I am *so thankful* you decided that being a victim was a **mindset** and not a sentence or an absolute.

You made that day powerless against you by sharing your story and helping others share theirs. You gave your body the nutrients it needed to heal an auto-immune disease you fought for 10 years. You allowed yourself to fall in love, move to a different state and travel to 11 countries in under a year. You started your own business and finally understood what it felt like to accomplish something bigger than yourself. You lost someone close to you, but not before cultivating a bond so fierce, few could understand. You got married to a man who vowed to choose you, every day, for the rest of his life and always have a Chapstick for you in his pocket.

Your decision to not play the role of the victim allowed you to continue living the life you *deserved.* You refused to be defined by the actions of a man whose purpose was to strip away your control and dignity, because he had none. And now, you have been given the biggest blessing anyone could have dreamt; two beautiful and perfect baby girls.

They chose you as your mom because of your strength, power, and fearlessness. They also chose you because you embrace change within yourself, and you strive to be a better version of you, every day. They want to be encouraged to speak up, be loud, and be unwavering in their personal power. They will know to apologize to those they've hurt, but never feel obligated to be "the bigger person". Because they don't exist to make other people happy. They exist to BE happy and shine a light of authenticity to all they come across. And they will face adversity, as many women do throughout their lives, but they were born out of a warrior, and warriors they will be, because of you.

Love Always,

Me

About the Author

Mara Shultz is a published poet, writer, and blogger. Healing from a place of trauma is where she draws her inspiration. Experiencing healing herself through different alternative modalities has allowed Mara to help others when traditional methods have been unsuccessful.

She and her family reside happily in Glenwood Springs, CO, drawing on beautiful landscapes and nature to continue thriving.

Dear Alma Jean,

To the little girl, the teenager, the young unwed mom, the abused wife, the business woman, the friend, the lover, the grandmother and the great grandmother, the ageless being. The you, that lives in your soul. You are quite the package.

Who knew how the life you lived and loved as a young child would disappear. Yet, it was that foundation that stayed with you and gave you strength. It was the light that lit your path out of the darkness.
The love, security, validation and happiness you were surrounded with when you were young was transformed by life into very difficult years.

Surviving so many abusers and rebuilding your life was challenging, but you did it. You didn't just survive; you still live with an open heart in spite of the pain you endured at the hands of others.

We never seem to have just one abuser. The abuse, betrayal, being disrespected and demeaned seemed never ending. You thought you would recognize and avoid another abuser, but you didn't. They come in many disguises. The next one was smarter, more manipulative, and harder to see as an abuser. The next, was even more difficult to recognize. No one else could see it.

He almost destroyed you. You were more broken than you thought possible. Every last tiny bit of your innocence that you had left was shattered and disappeared. But you rose from the pain and disillusionment, you learned how strong and how kind and full of grace you were. You never lost your desire to help others. You remembered who you were when you came into this world and chose to be that person. To not be the person that your abusive relationships could have turned you into.

Know, that there are things you couldn't protect yourself or your children from. It is not your fault! Your mind could not conceive of the horrible and disgusting behavior others were capable of. You are not responsible for the selfish and damaging behavior of others.

Being a kind, caring, loving and compassionate person left you vulnerable. It is hard to accept that there are people in the world that commit disgusting acts of abuse, just to pump up their own ego. They are damaged souls.

You learned to recognize the many faces of an abuser, and still stayed true to yourself.
What I love most about you, is your kind heart and your willingness to step up and denounce injustice and bullies. Helping others find their strength and their sense of self is your gift. Staying true to yourself and doing what is right, even when the price is high. Integrity matters to you.

It has been a life of fairytales and horror movies. The highs so high that it took your breath away from the sheer gratitude you felt for such an amazing life. The lows so low you felt your soul shatter and it felt as if your soul was bleeding out onto the earth. What saved you was your love of life and the determination to not let someone, anyone, destroy the soul that God placed on this earth with the purpose to make life better for everyone. You are stronger and more aware of how others struggle, because of your own experiences.

Forgiveness is a huge part of becoming emotionally strong. Forgiving others was easier than forgiving yourself for your lack of knowledge of the evil that exists. Accepting your own imperfections and lack of that knowledge is what gives you the strength and heart to do the impossible.

I am so proud of you for not giving up, for remaining kind and loving. For living your life on your terms with joy and grace.

May you always count your blessings on your darkest days and celebrate them on your best days. Being grateful for the people you have had in your life, still have and those yet unmet makes your life a beautiful story. You are blessed and also a blessing.

Sincerely,

The one that knows you best

About the Author

Alma Jean is a 69-years-young woman that is also a mother, grandmother, great-grandmother, wife and business woman. She lives on a 127-acre organic farm and loves cooking, reading, and writing. She also designs and remodels homes. Her greatest love is to inspire others to remember who they were when they arrived, and to forget what others and life have told them they are.

Dear Self,

You have had quite a childhood, and adulthood actually as well. You were always very quiet, always tried to stay under the radar and was always a, "Yes person." You always let people talk down to you and took it, even as a kid. One time when the older student in middle school said you could join their club, you were vulnerable enough to go along with it. It wasn't a nice initiation. He said if you wanted to be in the club you would have to do something for him. You were distraught but didn't tell anyone. You wanted to but the words didn't want to come out and you were afraid you were going to get into trouble, or to get the other student in trouble. This wasn't the last time you let someone take advantage. It changed you. You were never able to say no to anyone. And you just went with the crowd and were a follower, not a leader. You were taken advantage of plenty of times and people used you. They knew you were quiet and a people pleaser, and they used that to their advantage.

You also let people talk down to you, get you flustered, made you apologize for things you didn't have to apologize for, and question your ability to make your own decisions. You let people make you feel guilty for saying no. People were able to insult you, then when they saw you upset, they apologized. You didn't realize at the time that this wasn't healthy for you. This seemed to be the trend throughout your teenage life and even adult life. Situations like the one in middle school happened a few times. Once with your dad's boss, once with your boss and coworkers, and the worst was with your uncle, because you didn't want to get him in trouble. Thankfully for that one you told your cousin, who you knew had a big mouth, and he was confronted. Of course, he gave the worst excuse "I was drunk." Sure, he was confronted, but the aftermath of the situation already took over. I was nauseous, confused, upset with myself, mad at him… a whole bunch of emotions set in all at once. You actually felt guilty saying you did something that caused him to think that you wanted him to touch you. This idea stayed with you as you grew into your dating years.

As you got older, you continued to give people power over you. Not only sexual, emotional as well. Put downs, cursed at, threatened, and getting me to a point that I was apologizing when they were the one who needed to apologize. This need to please set me up for doing things I didn't really want to do. But I never wanted to let people down, or they would say, "But you were leading him on," so I had to continue. Then afterwards, feeling guilty telling myself, "You are a bad girl!" And the Jewish guilt set in. You were never open with you parents about this because of shame. So, you kept it in. Let it stew inside.

When you met your future husband, you felt he checked off all the boxes! Good boy, didn't do drugs, cute, mama's boy. There were some red flags that were missed. He was all those things but he did have a way of treating you as if you were a child. Yelling or flying off the handle for stupid reasons and just being disrespectful, but then apologizing and it was all better. It was like this for a while, even after we got married. It wasn't every day, and there were amazing days. It wasn't his fault, he was just never taught how to talk to a woman, or he just felt that it was okay to put down because he heard it growing up — the talking down to or giving silent treatments. It doesn't justify it of course.

The verbal turned into physical eventually, or at least threatening to. As the years went on though, many years, you started to find your voice thanks to a few certain positive influences on you. You, to this day, never cursed back at him or to others who did it to you. You felt you were too good for that. You did start to speak your mind and make it clear that what they were doing isn't right and insisted that you weren't going to accept it, and y*ou* were the one insisting on the apology.

Self, I am so proud of you and how far you've come! You are demanding respect and change. You were successful in that! Things started to turn around and you started to get more respect and your power back! You are one strong-ass woman! You never let your past define you and never gave up. The thing that made you change was raising your three girls. You didn't want them to be taken advantage of or disrespected. You did feel guilty for them seeing the things they did or hearing things they didn't need to hear. To a point, it affected them all in different ways. They were smarter than you thought. You didn't think it was affecting them. That's one thing you do regret but you did show them that the past doesn't define you and it's never to late to turn things around. That is a valuable lesson and you are a great mom for that. Through everything you stayed positive and strong (on the surface) so now your three girls are strong, beautiful women!

Self, if I can give you a few words of advice and encouragement it would be to never regret your past experiences because the way you have grown and raised your three girls. It proves that you can overcome, and you taught your girls the same. It also helped when, unfortunately, something happened to one or two of your girls, you were able to tell her she wasn't alone and can relate and help her through. Although she had her own way of dealing with it.

So proud of you! Keep strong and keep positive! Don't change you are perfect the way you are! Don't let anyone tell you otherwise and if they do just block it out!

Love you,
Love Leah ♡

About the Author

This author opted to be anonymous, so we want to brag for her. Leah is an incredible person. She is an extremely talented, award-winning baker. She is a fantastic mother, and a community member. She is supportive of her family, her friends and has the kindest soul we've ever met. Thank you so much for your honesty, openness, and generosity in sharing your truth with us!

Dear Me…

Or should I say - Oh, dear me!

Nevertheless, I want to remind you first of that precious little girl you were. Curly blonde hair, big blue eyes and always plenty of curiosity and energy. You loved playing in the backyard with the hose flowing water all over the grass, trees, flowers, but mostly all over yourself. When people asked you where you got those big blue eyes you were taught to answer, "From my Daddy who is away fighting in the war…" Little did you know what that meant, nor did you know that you'd never see your daddy again.

But you were surrounded by lots of loving women, even the one who sternly accused your grandma of spoiling you when she rocked you in her arms for your nap. That woman was your mother. You overcame your mother's lack of emotional or physical affection by becoming self-sufficient. You became a very intuitive child, observant in ways that many children are not. As you grew, you continued to watch from afar, thinking about grownups' actions and inactions. Even as a toddler you began establishing your own understanding of life and the people around you. You began distinguishing yourself as an individual. You talked a lot and you were told you were overly emotional by those who were not empathetic. You only became more empathetic as a result.

You always were drawn to the people who were free with their feelings and who were outgoing in their love of children, birds, animals and plants. You were always drawn to those who you heard your mother and grandmother criticize. People who you saw as free spirits, unconventionally enjoying life. You developed a love of music from the grownups who sang around grandma's piano as she played with her 'good' left hand. You often held her crippled right hand and learned to feel that disabilities were not restrictions, but just something a person worked around, and still got things done. You learned compassion and patience from helping her with her shoes. You felt people deeply with your heart. You accepted the quiet caring Japanese gardener who had just come home to West Hollywood after fighting at the Battle of the Bulge. You called him Brother. You loved him like an uncle all the rest of his very long life.

As you grew up and moved back east you became more exposed to different people with different cultures and different levels of respect for little children. You saw your mommy and your new daddy experience trauma and just carry on. You experienced abuse, emotional neglect, sexual trauma and betrayal from those whom you should have been able to trust most - the only grownups in your life. Yet, you became more compassionate and empathetic. You began finding your voice in the voices of the crickets at twilight and translating their choruses into poetry of your own making. You learned to write the 17 syllable Japanese poetry format of haiku. You loved the simplicity of Japanese art and culture.

You began coming out of your shell by singing and dancing in live theater, Glee Club, performing Shakespeare and classical plays in the Thespian Society. You 'became' Joan of Arc in George Bernard Shaw's play. You found solace playing in the woods of your Connecticut home. You found that communicating with animals and nature were your ways of restoring your souls and being at peace when the rigid restrictions of a silent, tense home life were more than you could bear. You loved staying all day alone in the woods, or ice skating on the pond until your toes became frozen. You loved the magic your parents created for the holidays and the mystery of the candlelight services on Christmas Eve. And the mystery of Torah in Temple on Friday night during

Chanukah with your mom's best friend and her kind Jewish husband. You developed your own spirituality that became unique to you; A spirituality you tried to share with your mother. You learned she was not that person.

> You began learning how to become your own mother. You had to. As you grew you found your greatest joy and comfort in caring for others' small children until you became a mother yourself. Yet you yearned for physical affection and emotional warmth. You yearned for someone special who would see you for who you truly were beneath the now sophisticated facade you had adopted to protect your tender vulnerable spirit. You learned that through trusting the wrong people you were spiritually violated, physically violently damaged and betrayed multiple times, all before you were old enough to be considered a full-fledged adult. Yet you rallied. And even though you suffered and ricocheted from the traumatic and shocking turn of events in your young life, being a multi-rape and sex trafficking survivor, you found ways to find the lessons in your pain, renew your spirit, not give up hope and try to become a better more compassionate person. You still tried to believe in the core goodness of others. You began putting your poetry to music. You learned to play guitar and found an outlet for your inner feelings, your observations of life and those people you encountered on your journey.

Even as you became a Playboy Centerfold through someone else's vision of you, you maintained and sustained your grounding in the arts, social justice and motherhood.

You stood up for human rights. You marched in the streets with your beautiful little brown son, with his massive sixties' afro, on your shoulders. You marched for civil rights after experiencing bigotry within your own family and bullying from the police when driving as a mixed-race family. You marched for Peace and Love participating in the Hippy Movement in 1967.

Even though, through trusting, believing in and making the wrong choices in the men in your life you still held onto the things that mattered to your soul. You loved little children. You became the mother you never had. You took other people's children and cared for them as your own. You learned the agony of losing those children through separation and death. You found your authentic self in spite of all your ordeals as you returned to nature. You allowed yourself to be led on an uncharted path that gave you a family of people, another mother, whom you would never have otherwise known, and another child, a little girl, after the deep loss of your son. I am astonished that you even survived that. You allowed yourself to be loved by them, to learn from them, to love them back. You learned to accept and give unconditional love.

One blood relative, your beloved cousin, Annie, now gone from cancer was the only one in your family who never forgot who you really were, and retained faith in the person she always knew was still beneath the trauma-informed surface. She knew you loved books, learning, writing and always made good grades. You received the gift she gave you when she took you by the hand and registered you for community college, which set in motion your former love of education and put you back on an academic path in which you found positive reinforcement for your accomplishments at the end of each quarter. It provided you with structure and a new circle of friends who shared the same goals. You discovered you had not lost touch with yourself. You were humbled by the respect you earned from your professors because of your writing skills and your commitment. You felt as though you had grown taller and straighter. You were so proud of yourself. You felt independent and self-sufficient, and enjoyed being on your own with your new toddler daughter.

You were loving life at last. You found renewal. And in the end, you repaid the love by being there for your Annie through her illness until the end… as you had for your own mother who sadly left you on this earth with a final betrayal from beyond the grave. But regardless, you were a loyal, devoted, caring daughter to her and your stepdad until the last. You were, and are, a good friend.

As time went on you fell in love with someone again after a couple of disappointments along the way. Someone with whom you thought would be the husband you longed for, a good daddy to your little girl, the equal partner you wanted to spend your life with, but in him you again were shattered. He injured his back and was unable to work, so you got a part time job as a nursing assistant learning new skills. You discovered you were pregnant. He abandoned you twice during your pregnancy yet returned to stay through the home birthing of your second daughter. He began drinking heavily causing you to lose your beloved dairy goat herd and farm. Once again you lost everything, and had to camp out in the VW bus for the summer but still somehow rallied and reinvented yourself. When there was no money for food or heating fuel, you made posters for the super market window, spoke to the woman who owned the village art gallery to arrange for space to teach dance classes for children. It evolved into more classes for grown women and you found yourself living in a trailer in an orchard overlooking the Colombia River caring for a dear 85-year-old couple, as well, parents of one of your dance students. You were seeing the domino effect of your positive actions.

I am so proud of the way you always took things in stride and took every challenge with a "can do" attitude. You have always been able to take inventory of your strengths, reevaluate your talents to make them work for you and support your children - even under the most difficult circumstances.

When you decided to return to Los Angeles to your family so your children could know their grandparents and you could try to make peace with them, healing old wounds after you felt you were stable and well yourself, your partner abandoned you again. You were back in the city with country ways and skills and two wonderful little girls under ten years old. After wondering why on earth you ever left the Pacific Northwest with your parents not really as happy to see you as you thought they would be, you applied for welfare, food stamps and registered for the Registered Nursing program at the local college. You rallied again. You reinvented yourself again. You repurposed your life again.

In three very difficult years you received every scholarship and grant you applied for, finally graduating with an Associate of Science degree in Allied Health as a Registered Nurse at 42 years old. You, along with two men, a Vietnamese doctor and a well-seasoned nurse, received honors out of the entire class. Didn't you find it amusing to discover that you of all people should win the only award that Glendale Medical Center gave to one RN from each graduating class - Clinical Excellence in the Area of Mental Health? They said you had great insight! I wonder why? (chuckle)

After 34 years of working in Home Hospice Case Management supporting the terminally ill, you became an expert on death and dying. You had made peace with the loss of your first child by accepting all the near drown babies, and learned to accept that while you didn't wish your child to drown, it was better for him to go rather than be trapped in a mind/body situation in which he had no quality of life nor even awareness. Every challenge you took on through your nursing career allowed you to find more healing for yourself and provide more empathy for others.

Even as you stepped back into the world of Hollywood show biz and Playboy glamor in your fifties, you were more secure and had already established yourself with a professional respect and integrity so that you took your ever evolving roles in stride. You became a published writer, a working actor and model again, a talk show host on public TV and campus radio. You received awards for your work spearheading a radio station on campus. You gave a platform for women on your TV talk show to tell their stories of overcoming adversity and finding lives of fulfillment and healing. You seemed to have found your true calling at last.

It wasn't too many years later that you were called again to confront your painful past by speaking publicly about being raped by a famous comedian, Bill Cosby. It wasn't anything you wanted or intended to do but when the moment arrived you stepped forward to support other survivors and stand shoulder to shoulder with them for truth and justice. Children and old friends you had lost touch with in your youth found you again and you were reunited as circles of healing came together.

I continue to be proud of the way you stayed focused, joined forces with other survivors and activists to successfully abolish the statute of limitations on rape and sexual assault in California effective January 1st, 2017. You, along with your growing sisterhood of survivors kept your eye on the goal making your attacker accountable in a court of law. Even when he was released preemptively from prison, you continued to speak out in support of truth and justice and changing laws to support survivors of sexual assault.

Each time a survivor reaches out to you and entrusts their story of sexual assault and rape, you know you have made a difference. It reaffirms your belief that through service to others we are ourselves find healing. You know that by continuing to speak out in support of legal changes, as a trauma-informed mentor and muse you are on the path you were meant to follow. You are raising consciousness and hopefully making a better world for this generation and generations to come for your own children, your grandchildren and theirs.

These are the seasons of your life. As you become closer to the end of your life and reevaluate your journey you are beginning to see the circles and seasons come to their fullness of healing. This was your life's purpose. This is your legacy. I will never let you doubt your value in this life ever again… I forgive you for your failings. I understand that you did whatever you did with the understanding you had of life at the time, the support, or lack thereof, and with the tools you had at your disposal.

You did good, Woman… I love you.

With a song in my heart…

Victoria xo

About the Author

Victoria Valentino was a serious acting student in New York, born in Hollywood, raised in Connecticut in an artistic family. But when she became Playboy's Miss September 1963, it radically redirected her life and career.

In 1969, on the very day she celebrated the signing of her recording contract with Capitol Records, her six-year-old son drowned. Several weeks later, she was drugged, kidnapped and raped by Bill Cosby.

Ms. Valentino, now a media personality, keynote speaker activist and mentor to other sexual assault survivors, shared her eclectic journey of survival and healing in her memoir: <u>Dirty Diamonds: The Repurposed Life of a Playboy Icon and Cosby Survivor</u>.

Dear Me in 2020,

A few months ago, you tearfully told your therapist, "When I look back on that time, I don't know how I survived."

At the tail end of 2019 you started dating your best friend from college. You dated for a few months in 2013/2014 and broke up but continued to be close friends until after graduation when you went your separate ways. You got married young and he moved to Sweden to play soccer. But despite time and place, when it came to him, you always wondered what if. In 2019 you got divorced and you quickly rekindled your relationship with him. After only a few months of dating you have a clear memory of thinking to yourself that you had never been happier, that you finally had everything you ever wanted.

A few weeks later you were staring at the word Pregnant on a Clear Blue pregnancy test and you were ecstatic. You've always wanted to be a mom. In fact, it had been 3 years since you had an early miscarriage, which made that 8-letter word all the sweeter. You were so excited to tell him that you FaceTime-d him immediately and held the test up to the camera. You'll never forget the look of absolute terror on his face. The look he gave you is still seared into your memory today. You went back and forth with him for weeks. You so desperately wanted this baby. You kept telling him it would work, you both had good jobs, owned a house, and had family nearby willing to help. He told you over and over again how a baby would ruin his life, how he would pay any amount of money to make this 'problem' go away. You were so sick. You had terrible morning sickness and threw up every single morning alone with no one to rub your back and tell you it would pass. You saw your baby's tiny heart steadily beating during a 6-week ultrasound and your love deepened. You started a baby book and carefully mapped out baby's family tree. You bought baby's first onesie covered in tiny elephants and imagined bringing him or her home from the hospital wearing it. But he refused to acknowledge the baby. He never put his hand to your growing bump or gave input when you were choosing a daycare. I wish you'd known at 6 weeks, or 8 weeks, even 12 weeks that he wouldn't support you. But you didn't, your instincts told you to protect this growing baby no matter what and you couldn't fathom how he wouldn't eventually come around to wanting this baby as much as you did. At about 14 weeks you acknowledged the very real possibility that you would be a single parent. You asked him if he would pay child support without a fight. Would he acknowledge paternity immediately or would he force you to take him to court? He told you he didn't know and he'd decide when the baby was born. Something snapped in you. You didn't want your baby to grow up without a loving and supportive father. You didn't think you could handle the stress of fighting for child support for 18 years. You worked so hard to get your professional license and a job with growth opportunities and you didn't know how you'd balance being a single mom with a demanding career. So, you gave in to him and called an abortion clinic. They were booked out two weeks. You would be 16 weeks pregnant when the procedure took place. You cried for hours every single day of those two weeks. In the middle of the work day, you would burst into tears and call your mom or him and just silently sob. You slept at your parent's house because you couldn't manage to be alone. You hardly ate, and what you did eat you threw up. In fact, the only time you felt at peace was while you were throwing up because you felt you deserved the pain. Mom told you she had never seen so much sadness in one person.

The night before the abortion you got a call from the clinic. State law had recently changed and abortions could only be performed up to 16 weeks. You'd be exactly 16 weeks on the day of the procedure, but the nurse warned if your baby measured any larger, they would not be able to perform the abortion. Was it a sign? Was the universe trying to tell you to keep this baby? But after two painful weeks of waiting, you knew you had to do it. He drove you 5 hours across state lines that night for an early morning appointment. You cried the entire time you were at the clinic. You couldn't look at the ultrasound. If you did, you knew you wouldn't go through with it. Baby measured at 16 weeks and 5 days on the day of the procedure.

It's been almost 2 years and you still haven't forgiven yourself and maybe you never will, not completely. There is a part of you that acknowledges that even if you were a single mom, you would have found a way. But I need you to know that the reason you made this decision was because you were put into an extremely hard position by someone you thought loved you. He forced your hand by depriving you of love and support, and leaving you to navigate the unknown alone. I know you worry that when you try to have a baby in the future, you won't be able to get pregnant; you feel like you don't deserve it after the choice you made. But you do deserve it. You deserve to be a mom; you've sacrificed a lot to give your future babies a life of love and familial and financial stability.

Perhaps the greatest act of self-love you've ever done for yourself was to leave him. It wasn't easy. After years spent wondering what if and the absolute bliss you felt with him before the pregnancy, you had never considered the possibility of not being together. But you couldn't forgive him for not supporting you and the baby. You didn't want your baby's life to have been lost in vain. You promised yourself if he put you into the situation to get an abortion, you would eventually leave him.

An act self-care you started after the procedure was working out. You had not worked out since high school when you were on the soccer team. You joined a gym and twice a week you went to a group fitness class. When you ran sprints on the treadmill and were sure your lungs would explode, you thought of your baby. You told yourself that if you could live through aborting a child you desperately wanted, then you could get through this sprint. And you know what else happened at the gym? You met your future husband. He was your coach and although you were still raw with pain from the past several months, you gave love another chance.

You've also become an advocate for abortion. You were always pro-choice but you didn't really understand what that meant. You found acceptance through education. You watched documentaries, read articles and books, joined a support group, and listened to podcasts. Your favorite book on the subject is *You're the Only One I've Told* by Meera Shah. You devoured the book searching for an abortion story that resembled you own so that you wouldn't feel so alone. While no single story was mirror image of yours as you'd hoped, you realized that 35% of women have been in your shoes.

You find peace by donating to the abortion clinic where you had the procedure on the anniversary of your abortion in honor of your baby.

Writing this letter was also an act of self-care. A few months ago, you read a quote by Brené Brown that stuck with you, "One day you will tell your story of how you overcame what you went through and it will be someone else's survival guide." If this letter can help even just one reader, then it was worth sharing.

Love,

Talia in 2022

About the Author

This author opted to remain anonymous, so we wanted to brag for her. Talia is a brilliant, compassionate person whose energy literally fills a room. She is fun-loving and compassionate, and really cares for the people around her.

When she first shared this story with us, it was before Roe v. Wade was overturned, and she was extremely cautious about who she shared this with. Luckily, she was comfortable finally sharing this story.

However, after the overturning of Roe v. Wade, she has been more vocal, sharing this story more, and how that Supreme Court Ruling is a dangerous regression in our country's rights and freedoms.

She is a brave, bold, incredible advocate and we couldn't be more honored that she felt comfortable sharing this experience with us.

Dear Me,

I knew you would want to know about the woman who you wondered if you could be. I am you and you are me. One day you will become more than you ever dreamed life could offer someone like you.

To the woman who still feels like a girl,
who thinks she has so much confidence but doesn't,
who can't see herself free from addiction,
who can't believe she was living her worst childhood nightmare.
To the girl who believed she broke everything,
to the woman who wondered where she belonged or fit in,
to the woman who wondered why she saw so much death but was somehow still alive.
To the survivor who learned so much on her own before smart phones were a thing.
To the woman who stood up for what she believed in but also did a lot of things she didn't.

You still feel like a girl. And it's not because you aren't a woman. It is simply because you never learned that adults were safe, so you never found comfort in becoming one yourself. You are the woman you needed back then.

You think you have confidence because you were taught that not being confident was weak. You don't actually have confidence in much of anything except you know you confidently have to fake your way through being confident to survive. Think about someone that you would consider, "Out of your league," and you'll see what I mean. Can you wrap your mind around the clean-cut person with money being interested in you? I know you can't because it was so deeply ingrained in you that, that is all anyone was interested in. Not your heart, your passion, your soul, your mind, your values, or your personality. The true way to find real confidence is through doing the inner work. Start learning about yourself through therapy, self-development, and spirituality as much as you can.

I remember the days when you would wake up and ask yourself if this addiction would ever end. You dream about a life without drugs or alcohol, and cannot even fathom living in such a way again. Deep down you know you are special, but the thing that makes it even more special is, you feel guilty that you think you are special. Every junkie walking this Earth wanted to feel special and loved and helped. What makes you any different or deserving of a different life? What makes you special is the purpose God has for you. There is nothing wrong with that! And that pull you've felt when you've looked around and wondered, "How did I get here?" is not a coincidence. You are a fighter, a winner, a leader. This is just another part of your testimony and story. It does get better.

To the woman who has just realized she has passed down a generational curse by mistake and there is no way around it, you did the best thing you could have done by leaving him for good. The kids will thank you for it later. You didn't break the relationship; it was never whole to begin with. He was never who you thought he was, and never will be. He wore a mask, used you when it was convenient for him, and slid right on back into the picture when you were weak. That's all there is to it. Let. It. Go. And try to heal as best you can.

You will never fit in perfectly anywhere because you were made to stand out. You are naturally what people told you, you never could be. You do it effortlessly and beautifully. You are an artist and your grandfather was wrong. Your mind never wants to stop learning because you want more out of life than just living check to check and being divorced by age 30. Not that there's anything wrong with that, but you've always been a dreamer. A visionary. Don't you dare let that gift go to waste.

You are incredibly resilient and smart. You find answers and silver linings when there are barely straws to grasp at. Don't underestimate yourself and look at what all you have lived through, thrived through, and beat the odds against just so far. And you did that all from your own emotional intelligence. If you didn't know, you found a way to find answers. If you had nowhere to go, you found a way to make where you stood feel comfortable. Your mind will always be the most important thing you will ever own or invest in, so make it count. Take care of it and it will take care of you.

To the woman who was so strong but has felt like such a hypocrite at times, would it have felt better to go back and choose the alternative? Would you have suffered less? Would others have suffered less? Play out how it would've gone for real. God loves you no matter how badly you think you have messed up.

What's all this God talk and talk about "Purpose?" Yes, you actually grow to embrace this amazingly attuned spiritual being that has been there inside of you all along. To the woman reading this, know that this is not the life that was planned for you. You can feel it deep down in your soul. Maybe somewhere along the way you learned that you couldn't even trust your own instincts, but you are literally entitled to live a happy and abundantly full life in every sense.

There is so much goodness out there waiting for you to accept it. I've become who you thought never would be. I'm on the other side. I'm doing it. You're doing it. I am you and you are me. I knew you would want to know about the woman who you wondered if you could be.

Sincerely,
Megan

About the Author

Hi there, beautiful human! I am so excited to be a part of this book and am so thankful and proud of you for picking it up. I'm a 37-year-old mom of two kiddos plus two fur babies and my love of helping people heal through photography started about 3 years ago. It has been a wild ride to get here. I've worked so many "jobs" in my life but I always knew there had to be something…. more. I have a feeling that if you're reading this, you've felt that way too at some point or another.

I like to tell people that I didn't find photography, but that it found me and that's really what it felt like. Once I discovered how helpful boudoir was for women looking for more in their lives too, I became so addicted to it. As a survivor of emotional, physical, sexual, and narcissistic abuse, boudoir is all about helping women see themselves as they truly are- beautiful, powerful, and worthy of REAL love.

Conversely, my love for fine art child portraiture aims to help women who want to break the cycle of abuse or neglect for their children and generations to come. So many of us have had these cycles of abuse handed down from our parents and have unknowingly been passing some of the same behavior and thought patterns down to our children. It's time to break the cycle. It's time to educate ourselves and our families. This ends with us right now.

I hope you gain some insight from our stories here and continue to search for new ways to love yourself.

--- *Megan Renee*

Dear Sarah,

When I met my husband–to-be, I was "taken with him" immediately! I was 15 years old and he was 2 years my senior. He seemed such a "man of the world"! He was the first boy I made out with and though I felt a bit defiled the first time he explored my body; it was definitely exciting! We would go to his parent's basement and do some really heavy petting. I wanted to be a virgin when I was married, so we stopped at the critical point! He agreed with my goal and I really respected him for it.

His parents were fantastic and really welcomed me into the family, as they did not have any girls! I adored them. They were very well-to-do, unlike my parents who had to be careful with their money. When we got married, after my undergraduate degree, my mother-in-law would take me to luncheons and fashion shows! I was in "seventh-heaven". My own mother worked full time as an educator, and I never really got to hang out with her, except as my Girl Scout leader. My dad was a dentist and I worked in his office as a receptionist before college and during summers.

My mother-in-law kowtowed to my father-in-law's desires and put up with his denigrating attitude toward her. He was the king of the house, although this was not unusual for most households in those days. She paid a price for being pampered! Looking back, that is where my husband got his expectations! My parents were very egalitarian. When my father-in-law had a stroke, my training as a speech pathologist really paid off and he would come to visit so that I could work with him to recover his speech. He adored me and the feeling was mutual.

 My husband and I both wanted me to be a stay-at-home mom… me, because I never had one and, he, because he always had one! I did help him with his business, soldering his printed circuit boards and answering phones in his engineering business from our home. I also volunteered singing and playing my guitar at my children's elementary school when they were enrolled. I was a president of the PTA 4 times, as well as holding every other PTA office at least once! When his business grew, he felt he needed an office away from our home and he got a friend of ours to be his secretary. He ended up having an affair with her and I was appalled as she was such a "good friend". Her husband named mine as cause of their divorce, although at the time I thought Jeff was crazy. As I discovered later, this was the first of many subsequent affairs for my husband. I was clueless, as none of my friends or family ever cheated on their spouses!

When our eldest son was ready to go to college, my husband needed me to work to help make money for the tuition. Because I had so many contacts in the community through my volunteering, I got a terrific job with the Kohl Education Foundation, as Director of Programs and Services for the Kohl Jewish Teacher Center. My husband said he would pick up the slack with the kids on the weekends that I would be working or traveling. Needless to say, he did not follow through.

After a while, Harvey told me he didn't love me and I asked that we go to a marriage therapist. It did not work, unfortunately, as he refused to tell the truth at therapy. The therapist told me this later, when I was so confused at the outcome. I kept trying to make our marriage work, but he was more and more distant. We were at a close friend's house for a party, when I asked to go home when it had gotten late. He spoke to me with such distain that, when we got home, I told him that a person did not speak to someone he loved in that manner. I said that we needed to go back to therapy. He replied that he would not do that again, as "he was who he was" and that was that! We agreed to have a divorce and that it would be "amicable". Amicable meant that we would share a lawyer and we would divide the assets equally. Of course, that was nonsense! He fiddled with the books and made it seem that we earned equal amounts of money, so no alimony, of course!

An example of his callousness, was when I was on my way to be with our daughter in California, as she was undergoing surgery for an elbow injury. He called me in the taxi to tell me that he had cancelled my credit cards and I did not have any money! I was hysterical, to say the least! My eldest son did not want to hear about this, as he said he needed to keep a good relationship with his father. That was important for me to hear, once I had gotten over the hurt of that statement, because it was reality that my kids needed two parents, not just one. That created a plan for me to follow in the years to come! Our children never had to worry about he and I being in the same room together, even when he married his last mistress!

Speaking of her, before we divorced, he suggested we get a separation. I thought this was a good idea and then discovered that he went to live with his mistress! I was so furious, that I changed the message on our answering machine to say that this was the _____ home and if they wanted to speak to him, he was at his girlfriend's house and they could call him there. I gave her number.

Our friends were hysterical when they called our phone number and heard the message. Word of it traveled like wildfire and soon reached my husband's attention. He was furious and demanded that I change the message and of course I didn't! Small victories.

I did go to a divorce support group at the local YWCA and it was really helpful to hear how others handled their divorces!

Some of them actually made me laugh! One of the women, who had a huge house and swimming pool, etc. threw all of her husband's clothing into their swimming pool and cemented it over. I really loved hearing that. Talk about revenge! They did help me know where to open a bank account and checking account and how to handle those details. I never handled our money, as that was my husband's bailiwick. They also gave me the name of an excellent woman divorce attorney. My youngest child was a senior in high school when we got divorced. We had been married 33 years.

My mother-in-law and I got together every Thursday and visited the Chicago Botanic Gardens. Then we would all go out to dinner before she drove home. Later in our marriage, she became very ill and when we were getting a divorce, I used to go visit her, as she was bed-ridden. My father-in-law had passed away and she was alone except for a housekeeper. As she got more and more debilitated, my husband decided that I could not visit her. I believe that his lawyer or his brother thought that I might try to get a share of the family money as I was like a daughter to her. Such a rotten thing to do to his mother, but typical of his narcissism! I did visit her in the mausoleum every week and I brought her and Dad flowers.

After our divorce, when I realized that I needed to get medical benefits, I got a terrific job at a synagogue in Wrigleyville and after a year, I sold the house and bought a condo 10 minutes from where I worked. I was able to use my talents to build up the school and even acted as the Director of Adult Education for the synagogue as well! I worked at that job for 10 years, until they replaced me with a rabbi. I then taught and was Religious School Director at other synagogues in the Chicago area. I became very confident because I had a lot of successes. I had a terrific reputation in the Chicago Jewish educational community. One of the other principals once introduced me as the most creative Educational Director/teacher in the Chicago Jewish community! I was a leader in Chicago's CAJE Conference.

In addition to Religious School work, I also worked as a facilitator with the Anti-Defamation League's "A World of Difference" program. For 25 years, I helped teachers and students in the public and private schools learn how to be allies and how to handle bullying and bullies. It was fabulous work, but it ended with the Black Lives Matter riots.

What I have discovered looking back on my life, is that when you have talents and intelligence, do not let anyone denigrate them. That is what narcissists try to do. Stay strong in your gifts and create a better world with them. That is why they were given to us!

Love,

Me

About the Author

This author opted to remain anonymous, so we wanted to brag about her for her. Sarah is an incredible person. She loves to garden, educate children and inspires others to keep growing. She is one of the kindest and most nurturing people that we've ever met, and we adore her so much.

Her generosity and kindness is limitless and she changes the dynamic of every room she walks into. She is a warm, nurturing and loving person, and we are so honored that she felt comfortable enough t share her story with us. Thank you so much for inspiring, nurturing and loving people into growth and healing. We adore you.

Dear Kimmie,

When you look back on your life at my age, 60, you discover things about yourself you never considered a possibility, let alone reality.

My abuse began around age four or five, by a cousin that threatened me with parental abandonment if I ever told. A great asset for the abuser of an adopted kid. That seed was the subsequent reason I became fair game for many more abusive relationships throughout my life, because I thought that's what grown-ups did, that's what was expected of me and "kids were to be seen and not heard," no matter what the circumstances.

Not only did I endure my own experiences of abuse as a child, but from the age of sixteen, I also held the secrets of my high school sweetheart, who was groomed for abuse by a very jealous priest. Ours was a relationship founded on similar pains and rescues. He held me through psychological terrors, made me feel loved and kept an abusive neighbor at bay. In turn, I gave him a safe place to share his pain, showed him what unrelenting love was and gave him a solid reason to tell the priest to go to hell, a sentiment that didn't go over well because he retaliated with vengeance.

After several years, he fell to insurmountable pressures and broke up with me but we remained devoted friends and continued to share and keep each other's secrets until his death. It was that relationship in part that gave us both the strength to eventually and independently expose our abusers. Unfortunately, the damage was done and the aftermath has been as difficult as the trauma to navigate.

While he used and abused alcohol to cope, I have tried everything but drugs and alcohol; writing, meaningless sex, celibacy, bad relationships, books, massage, yoga, church, God, talk therapy, exercise, more books, self-admission to a facility, more bad relationships, more writing, lectures, movies, music, dance classes, art, college, travel, MDMA therapy and finally hypnosis. While the aforementioned all helped to a degree, eventually the weight of depression would rear its ugly head and lead me down the path of self-disillusionment and disgust. Had I known hypnosis would have led me to the calm, peaceful place I'm currently basking in, it would have been my first choice, not my last resort. I can't recommend it enough, but only with a professional therapist. That said, as I look back on my life with clarity and kindness, the same kindness I've always applied to others but never myself, I can honestly say, I'm bad-ass! And so are YOU!

Your life seemingly turned on a dime, but you have the power to turn it back and right the ship. The same strength you've had to stay alive until today, to get out of bed, brush your teeth, drink a glass of water, get dressed, to pick up and read this book … is all you need to pull YOU through and out of the darkness.

No matter how low the feelings have been, how many times you've found yourself in the gutter of your mind, NO ONE HAS BEEN ABLE TO END YOU. And that's because YOU ARE BAD-ASS!

It means that while you've been unable at times to see your way out, you still did! You always will! And you will continue doing so because innately, intuitively and ultimately, you know you're worthy of way more than this ugly world has provided.

With every fiber of your being, you know you're infinitely amazing and if given the chance, you'll prove it! So, PROVE IT! But ONLY to YOURSELF because that's who matters.

Symbolically and/or actually invite the bastards to go to hell. Annoy them mercilessly by living another day ... then another and another until the days run into weeks, into months, years, decades.

As long as you're alive, they will never rest. Staying alive means, you live rent free in their twisted minds for the rest of their lives because they'll never know if and when you'll open your mouth and expose them for the grotesque creatures they truly are. They have everything to lose, you have everything to gain. Not knowing if and when exposure is near is a powerful tool to wield and you should wield wildly every chance you get! You, my friend, HAVE ALL THE POWER!

If you're reading this, then you're well aware of how powerful internal torment can be, how it can ruin your sleep and eating habits, relationships, employment, etc. You may not feel safe enough to expose them, but that doesn't matter. You can ruin their lives easily. The best way to abuse your abuser is to stay alive, and just for fun, piss in their Cheerios by being happy while doing it.

They'll pretend to have a good life, post photos of kids, family, and travel on social media, but their reality remains a constant walk on egg shells wondering if and when you'll expose them. If you really want to torture them, live a very long, happy life!

When the weight of sadness, the feelings of hopelessness, thinking yourself unlovable ... when the racing thoughts run so closely together you can't sleep or catch your breath, remember YOU HAVE ALL THE POWER!

Love,
Me

About the Author

Kimmie Dee is an incredible writer, stand-up comedian, and general bad ass. She doesn't take crap from anybody, and that's what makes her so captivating. Her Jersey roots shine through her tiny, fireball exterior, and she sends people into stitches with every witty one-liner.

Kimmie is the owner and operator of No Indoor Voices, a company that brings comedy shows, musicians, writers salons and general debauchery to Santa Barbara, CA.

She's a world traveler and endless explorer.

Dear Melinda,

Gosh, it has been a long, hard, upward battle to get to where you are today. When I think about all the toxic people I allowed into your life, people that created more trauma for you; People I allowed to use your body for sexual gratification; The disgusting people I allowed to abuse your body physically and mentally. I allowed them the power to break your heart and sometimes your body into pieces, like a glass shattering on a floor. And every time you would try to pick up the pieces these toxic people left of the ground and heal, I would bring another toxic person around you that wanted to take more pieces of you.

I know a lot of times you would feel so empty inside because I allowed so many people to hurt you. I never gave you the time you needed to learn to love yourself first, and to heal those broken bits of yourself. For that I'm truly sorry. You deserved better.

I can't help but feel shame when I think about the choices, I made that brought heartache, damage, and trauma. I'm sorry I filled your body with drugs and liquor and cigarettes to try and feel whole and to deal with our trauma. I'm sorry I let the things our abusers said live inside your head rent-free. In doing so, it drove your mind crazy to the point of self-harm and no longer wanting to live. For that, I'm very sorry I started abusing your mind and body when no one was around to do it anymore. I'm sorry I have always put everyone and their feelings first, above what was best for you -- even when I knew you were overwhelmed and shouldn't do these things. I'm sorry for not believing in you, and not valuing you or having respect for you, and the things you have been through. I'm sorry I have not demanded others treat you with care, love and the compassion you deserved.

When I think about who I am writing this letter to, it is you as a small child being born into abuse and neglect, by parents that were both born and raised in traumatic homes. As much as I think they both truly wanted to be different for their children, it was a very real and hard struggle for them to try and break those generational cycles. They failed in some aspects, were successful in others, and failed miserably in other areas. But as a 9-year-old, you felt like your mother drew happiness from your pain any way she could. She never wanted you to have physical affection. Her punishments were way beyond the other children. She dragged your siblings into everything to get them angry with you, isolate you, and make them not want you around. She wanted you to know you were worthless every chance she could, and blamed you for everything all the time.

Your father was drinking heavily, and let his temper take control when disciplining you. I remember how when he beat you with that extension cord you tried to get away but his grasp was too strong. You felt helpless and sad and angry. You felt hopeless. But the strongest feeling was confusion. You were confused why he was whooping you so hard and why he wasn't stopping. I remember screaming out loud because it hurt so bad when he hit me. I remember the sting on my skin as it welted and tore open. You were terrified of him when he was angry. I remember how much you loved them and just desperately wanted them to love you back. I remember you as a child wondering if you still loved them even though they hurt you. And why couldn't they forgive you for being born, and for messing up -- or what they decided was messing up. For years I resented you for needing their love, affection or approval because it made you weak, and gave them access to your heart, that they shattered over and over again.

This letter is to 18-year-old you that met a man who would carry on the abuse that others had inflicted upon you. I remember the first time this man that was supposed to love you, backhanded you in the mouth after just a month of being together. I remember the salty taste of the blood in my mouth as it filled. Most importantly, I remember you sitting there not even realizing that what he was doing was wrong. You knew it hurt and you were afraid, but by this point you thought these things were normal and that this was love. You always felt that if you loved these abusive people enough, they would change. But it didn't happen. They remained the same and you continued to deprive yourself of the unconditional love you gave to them.

This man abused you and got you pregnant. You experienced loss after loss, and the last one you almost bled to death because you wanted to make him happy, and thought that if you had his child, it would change him. But he repaid you by impregnating another woman and hiding it for 6 months until you found out on your own. You were devastated and angry with yourself and felt like a failure instead of seeing him for the narcissistic, manipulative monster he was.

You continued to give love to him and allowed him to continue breaking your heart, and gave him pieces of yourself that you would never be able to get back. You told yourself if you just tolerated the beatings, gave him children and stayed when he cheated, he would see how much you loved him and he would change and love you the way you so desperately wanted. But it wasn't meant to be.

One day after 15 years and another affair, you decided to leave because when you looked at him, you were disgusted. You had endured all these things trying to prove your love for him and stayed because of your children, but you had finally had enough. You didn't want your sons to think it was okay to treat a woman that way. They watched me accept abuse as treatment. I didn't want my daughter to grow up thinking that a man hitting her, disrespecting her, and belittling her was acceptable behavior from her partner because she deserved better than I did. And my boys deserved better than I did. So even when I left, it was because I loved them more than myself, and I could not bear to think they would treat someone or allow someone else to abuse them because of the example I had set in front of them.

I walked away. I stood on my own. I got a job working all the hours I could because I didn't have a high school diploma. The divorce judge split custody 50/50 with him. He had never abused the kids so I felt that they would be safe. I literally did everything I could, as usual, to get along for them, and still allowed him control me.

On October 4, 2015 when our daughter 12, she disclosed the abuse her father had done to her. At that point I nearly broke. I was so angry and sad, and felt guilty -- like I should have known. I felt completely worthless. It took several months to get him in prison where he belonged, and I had no choice but to fight because my child couldn't. She was too young, so I fought tooth-and-nail to get him to prison and keep him there. I channeled that anger, sadness and guilt into determination and to drive me to help other parents. I created a group where parents of abused children could lean on each other for support and not feel alone.

Then I started working on giving myself some grace. I worked on understanding why I'm so guarded and did the hard work to heal and treat you the way you deserved to be treated. I started working on my self-worth and trying to get those negative, intrusive thoughts you had been told your entire life out of your head. It was a long, hard journey to understand your worth and value as a human being because starting as a young child, people treated you like you didn't have value or deserve love. I noticed that, when I met the amazing man I'm married to, when he would hug me, I would tense up and it hurt his feelings. He thought he was doing something wrong. I had to learn that what he was doing was normal, but how my mind and body responded was not normal. It was a constant reminder of how broken I was and how badly I needed to fix these broken pieces of myself because I was worth it.

I was learning that I was worthy all the love and dedication I had given to people. That if I would focus on loving myself and healing myself and giving myself the time, energy and love that I deserved, then I could start to heal little by little.

I want you to know Melinda, more than anything else, that you are just as important as everyone else in the world. You deserve just as much love as you give to others. You are beautiful and strong, and have survived so many things that you shouldn't have had to. But guess what, you did, and you're still standing strong, and still growing stronger every day.

Furthering your education while being the best mom you can be. You are compassionate and loving, kind and have a huge beautiful heart. You are one of the bravest people I have ever known. And although you're still in the process of working on all these things, which is why this letter has been so hard for me to write, I'm choosing to heal and help. I'm learning it's okay to say No sometimes. I'm learning it's okay to do things to refill my battery. I'm learning I'm worthy of love from other people, and that not everyone in the world is out to hurt me.

The feeling of being completely free is indescribable. I want you to know, Melinda, that you still have a lot of life left. So go out there make a lot more memories. Have fun and show the world what you have to offer.

I love you always, and just know that every day will not be a great day but you will get through it and experience the sunny days that are just around the corner. You beat the odds in a deck stacked against you, and if you can do that, you can take a few rainy days.

"You must learn to trust that there is a future waiting for you that is beyond what might be able to grasp at this present moment."

Love,

Melinda Prince

About the Author

My name is Melinda Prince. I'm 44-years-old, married to my incredible husband, Michael, and we have 5 amazing kids. My children are everything to me. I'm working hard to change generational cycles of abuse.

I'm a survivor of S.A and D.V. and Child Abuse. I'm a warrior who fought for my life. My family has been through a lot of very difficult things, and we still have ups and downs, but we are all still getting on with life and succeeding. We have learned a lot from our trauma and just want to help others. That's why you're reading this letter, and it's only a small piece of my story.

I wanted to show it's never too late. You're strong enough, even on that day when you're down and think you can't get back up. You can, I promise. I'm living proof you can.

I'm currently enrolled at the Mo Goodwill Excel Program to get my high school diploma, and I'm set to graduate in December. I am ambitious. My goal is to pick a career and at the same time, write legislation to change the way the legal system handles child sexual assault. The laws are way too lenient, the system is very flawed, and focuses more on perpetrators instead of victims. That must change. And I'm bringing an army with me to ensure it does. I have amazing teachers that are making sure I have the best education to do so. I run an amazing support group on Facebook for parents whose children have experienced sexual assault.

I would like to thank my husband and children for their unconditional love and support.

I would like to thank my sister for always being my rock as a child. Without her, there is no me.

Finally, I would like to thank my teachers at the MO Goodwill Excel Program for believing in me and giving me your time and encouragement.

Dear Logan,

I guess we all have to go through our major "thing" in life, but it was a long road, and you came out on top after two plus years. You dealt with a very confusing combination of gaslighting, deception, infidelity, and adultery in all its forms. I know it completely changed your views of the world and the people in it. I know it made you question every relationship you had in your life. I know it to this day makes you have your shields up at all times.

BUT, it also gave you the ability to grow and become that much wiser. It gave you the ability to love and empathize with others more greatly. It gave you the ability to help those going through similar things, and it gave you the ability to actually live your life for yourself.

I know everyone thought you were going through heartbreak, but in reality, it was navigating the betrayal, disrespect, and logistics. I know you were in a place where you would wake up somewhere that wasn't your home, and wondering what you did to end up there. You would question your self-worth, not only as a husband, but as a friend. Dating would be virtually impossible, because you wouldn't open yourself up. Everything had an expiration date. Trust was nearly impossible.

The good news is that time literally does heal all wounds. You've grown and become a better man. You dove headfirst into your career and creative endeavors, which yielded so many more opportunities. You've made some amazing friends along the way. A few have even become more than friends. You're allowing yourself to date and get out there again. You've learned to focus on experiences instead of expectations.

More importantly, you've shown that with the help of your friends, you can get through anything. It wasn't easy but you have come so far in two years. The world is yours for the taking. And like we always say, "Onwards and upwards."

You got this.

All the Love,

Logan 2022

About the Author

This author opted to remain anonymous, but that shouldn't exclude the fact that Logan is an absolute example of morality, humility and grace. Despite the adversities faced in his life, you can find him working hard at everything he does. Constantly giving back to friends, family and his community with a smile, and never expecting anything back. From humble beginnings, to adversity, to recovery; From losing everything to rebuilding his world, Logan has never changed the person he is, because the person they are is hands down AMAZING.

Dear Wanda,

You were stuck in purgatory Hell for decades. You felt like your life was a sham. You faked being okay on the outside, but on the inside, you were screaming, "Help me!"

You faked it for so long, numbing and blocking your real emotions and feelings, that over the years you began to lose all the real stuff. When you finally reached a place that you thought you could do something about it, you didn't know how. You had lost the ability to be real and didn't know how to ask for help.

You needed knowledge, skills, courage, belief and trust in yourself but had none of these things. You had lost so much by doing only what you had to do to survive. You had lost all courage, self-esteem and the ability to FEEL. You thought that learning how to block all the bad had to be better than living in such emotional pain.

For 16 years, you hated yourself. You felt that you were stupid for staying with your abuser and stupid for returning to your abuser, not understanding what you now know as your, "Why Roots."

When you were a teenager, you witnessed verbal abuse, threats and violence, so you thought that was normal.

The abuse you suffered at the hands of your abuser has negatively affected your life in devastating ways for over two decades. It has caused you to lose your self-esteem and confidence. It has caused you to have chronic anxiety and panic attacks, major depression and years of terrible suffering from PTSD.

You felt constantly afraid, ashamed and embarrassed of your past. You just wanted to forget it ever happened!

You thought, what good was it to dwell on the past? It is over and you can't change it. No matter what you did, what you tried or how busy you kept yourself, the nightmares continued, haunting you and controlling you.

Eventually hitting rock bottom, you gave up on getting better and just accepted doom and gloom as, "your life," never expecting to ever recuperate from your abuser's corruptions. You were damaged goods and you just had to accept it. This was as good as it gets, and you assumed that there was nothing better in your future. You just wanted to die… a lot! Suicide was thought of often.

You had barely escaped with your life, and yet, you continued, to hold "yourself" captive as the battered woman you had once been.

Through reading several self-help books and finding the right counselor you were able to tell yourself, "Judgments or not, I'm sick and tired of being afraid, ashamed and embarrassed of my past! I have literally lived in fear of my **past** for most of two decades, and it's time to shuck that unnecessary, heavy burden. We all have a past and no one is without sin. Judging a person by its weakest link is like judging the ocean's strength by just one of its waves."

Through self-love and building self-esteem you began to trust yourself again. I'm proud of you for learning to ***TRUST*** again. You learned that in order to trust someone else, you ultimately had to trust yourself, because if you don't even trust yourself, how can you trust others. For your healing journey to be successful you must reconnect with yourself first, before you can learn to trust someone else.

You also learned an important factor is that you need to work on your **self-esteem** which also increases your ability to trust. If you don't have self-esteem, you don't have self-worth. Nor do you have any confidence in your environment. You can't complete your healing journey until you've learned to trust yourself. Once you've learned to trust yourself, then you can learn to trust someone else. Self-esteem is a process that flows according to how a person's life is going. You learned that self-esteem can either strengthen you or destroy you. If you put yourself down, that has a direct effect on how you think and feel about yourself. You learned how to acknowledge when you were putting yourself down, by identifying negative self-talk then you can replace it with positive self-talk. I'm proud of you!

You learned that you had to _matter_ before you could get better. You had to learn to care about yourself before you could _trust_ anyone else to _care_ about you. It was then you saw how everything was connected.

You must trust yourself, in order to be able to trust someone else. You have to care about yourself before you can care about others enough to trust others to care about you; And for you to _let_ them help you!

And when you've learned to trust yourself only then will you be able to trust someone else. Trusting yourself is your biggest compliment because it means you _value_ yourself!

Wanda your pain was not in vain!

There _is_ a reason you went through what you did.

What your abuser intended as evil against you, God will use for good, to help others.

Your past does _not_ define you, but it came very close to destroying you! So now say to yourself, "I'm taking _my pain_ and turning it into _my purpose,_ and I'm taking back **my power!!**

With this quote from your counselor your life was forever changed:

> _"Well, it is a testament to how caring and how Intelligent you are that you still have a hard time accepting the fact that you took a human life, even though you were justified in doing so."_

Those words literally changed your life!!

The advice that I would give myself is to TRUST YOUR GUT!! If something doesn't feel right it's probably wrong. If it's too good to be true then it's wrong. If you have an uneasy feeling, trust it!

I love you Wanda.

You are a strong person that has been through hell and back. Your courage is amazing.

Be proud of yourself!

I Love You Wanda Parker

About the Author

Wanda Parker is a 3-time best-selling author of her Caught In A Web of Gaslighting series, available on amazon. She is a survivor, activist and powerhouse author who has taken the survivor community by storm. Her story is intriguing, filled with crazy twists and turns, and all true.

She is a mother and grandmother, and is very close with her family.

Dear Stacey (Age 32),

I know things seem so hard right now as you are not only in your darkest time but feeling so alone. You are smart, you are strong and you have a heart of pure gold.

You are so used to giving 100% when sometimes you just don't have anything to spare -- but you believe you are weak or worthless when you dare to use the word no, so you don't. If you only knew then what I know now, I could have told you things would change for the better. You always felt that if you ever showed the slightest ounce of vulnerability, you would be to blame. NONE of the things beyond your control were ever your fault. Your feelings are valid!! Nobody can take that away. Just because you feel a certain way doesn't mean you are being dramatic or over-sensitive, it means you are feeling and being real!

I have always struggled with self-esteem, self-worth and self-love. When you are surrounded by toxic, narcissistic people they will always try to keep you down, as that is the only way for them to rise above.

History repeats itself and as we learn and grow, we get stronger and more determined than ever. I know it has taken so much strength and courage to be where I am today, so that must mean I am stronger than I ever believed I was or ever could be. The darkest times make the light at the end of the tunnel more radiant than you could ever imagine. You deserve to be treated only with kindness and respect. Abuse of any kind is never acceptable and says nothing about who you are it only says something about who the abuser is.

You can accomplish anything you set your mind to. Use the negativity and doubt from others to fuel your ambition because you will prove them all wrong. We can't change our past but we can certainly learn from it to make our future a better place.

I am still a work in progress and think I always will be. I no longer expect perfection from myself, but I always strive for it. You can never fail if you keep trying. Through my years of experiences, I am learning to love myself and feel comfortable in my own skin.

Loving me and always doing what I feel is right is more important than needing others approval. The moral of my story is to always keep on keeping on because I am better than good enough!

Love,

Stacey (Age 54)

About the Author

This is Stacey's first co-author experience. She is looking forward to more opportunities to share her life experiences to help others.

Hi, Pete.

Dear Nana,

You're 19 years old and you have already experienced something I don't wish *anyone* ever gets to experience in their life. Life was about to unfold in new and unimaginable ways. Eventually to your benefit, however of course, you didn't see it that way whilst in the middle of the storm. There is hardly ever a feeling of brightness, when the only thing you see is deep, abominable, profound darkness all around.

You were a cheerful, joyful, free-spirited girl, full of possibilities and dreams. You felt unstoppable and most of all, you had the certainty that everything in your life had only one direction to go, *Up.* College life was fun. You left your home country, Venezuela, following your dad's footsteps, to go to Louisiana State University (LSU) as he once did. You met a man, fell in love and married him shortly after. Life was looking good. You were starting a new stage of life full of hopes. You moved from your adored town of Baton Rouge to New Orleans, because that's where your now husband worked. And once again you moved to a new place. You had already moved 11 times in your life because of dad's career, so it was no big deal to do it again, much less because this time it was your choice, your life, your love.

Then on a beautiful April afternoon a stranger dared to go into your house, wait for you to get back from school and take one of the most important values any human being can have. He took your faith, your sense of security, your pride, your peace, your dignity, and ultimately your soul. He violated you physically and emotionally. He left you there numb, detached, and for the first time in your life, feeling that death was a far better option than the darkness that began to come over you. Your four-month-old marriage began its journey towards its end. How could a marriage between a 19-year-old young woman and a 20-year-old man which had just started survive a rape?

The silence and the screams happening at the same time inside of me were overwhelming. I felt alone, no one in my family knew. I didn't want to share anything but I needed everything. Being an immigrant and not having long life friendships and very few family members close was extremely hard. However, at the same time this allowed me the quiet space I needed to find my own grounding. Dad called that same night when the police were still in the apartment. He rarely called me directly; it usually was mom. But he did. He found out. Shortly after, he came to visit. When he got to our apartment he said "Never thought your house would be so organized and nice. You were always a mess." We just looked into each other's eyes and smiled with teary eyes. We never spoke a word about what had happened. I was always grateful for his visit. Thank you for coming to visit me, Dad. It did mean the world to me.

Life was hard those months and years after. Being scared to walk into your own house is not something I had ever felt before, because usually you are fearful in the streets. However, I was afraid in my own home. My husband didn't know what to do or what to say to me. So days, weeks, months, would go by and we would say nothing. I sometimes wished he could have asked me more about what I was feeling. I understand now, it was too painful. I also later came to realize that's not who he was, nor who I was. We didn't like sharing our feelings. This was never apparent to me before.

My husband would make me run almost every day around the neighborhood in the hopes that we would see him, but nothing… Then one sunny day, maybe weeks or months later, I don't remember because everything was blurry, I saw him. Yes, I saw the man who raped me driving a car next to me. I will spare you all the details, but I was able to recognize him in a huge mugshot book the New Orleans Police

Department showed me at the precinct. That man was the owner of the car driving next to me, though he looked very different now from the picture. It was him. But the police said he had an alibi for the day of the "incident." How did they know, I wondered? They hadn't talked to him yet. "He is an undercover cop," the detective in charge of my case said. "It couldn't have been him." And these two young traumatized foreigners believed the story. The police here would not lie to us. Would they?

Life continued to be hard in that apartment. I was feeling more and more anxious every day. I was going to the rape crisis group in New Orleans, but that was not helping much. On the contrary I felt it made it worse, having to hear horror stories every week, many of them much worse than mine. So eventually I stopped going. I was depressed, constantly scared of any little noise in my house and my husband had to always announce himself, because if he walked up to me from behind, I would go into a panic attack.

So, we decided to move. He asked for a transfer to the office in New York and they approved it. We packed everything including my new guardian, a gorgeous trained German shepherd that had to bark telling me everything was okay, in order for me to open the door every time I got home. We left in the hopes that we could forget. We wanted to start a new life. And it worked. I felt safer in the streets of the dangerous New York pre-9/11, than in my old New Orleans home.

And why did it work? Well, it started way before the rape as I later realized. I had learned as a child to detach when I felt pain. That can be very useful not to feel. It worked during the rape. I went somewhere else and was able to literally numb myself and feel nothing. And that's what I began to do little by little, more and more. I detached and I was able to feel nothing, remember nothing. But of course, the scares and the pain were there, repressed, hidden needing to come out. I wish I would have shared it with my best friends, with my mother, with anyone. I know now that would have helped so much, but I didn't. I guess there was a feeling of shame and also not wanting to remember.

After graduation we went back to Venezuela and I decide to go to therapy to finally face my demons. It took 6 months before I spoke about the rape in the therapy. But that's when my healing process began. I finally told my mom what had happened and I got divorced from my husband.

The therapy helped me become aware of so many other problems I had, which had nothing to do with the rape, but became bigger and louder because of it. This then became the beginning of a lifelong journey of growth and healing I have followed ever since. I cannot say it has been easy because it has not. It has been a very hard and painful road. However, I can say without a shadow of a doubt, I would not be the woman I am today if it wasn't because of the abuse. The abuse made me look for the psychological and emotional help I needed to heal many other aspects of my life that were hurting too.

I believe I didn't get better because of one tool or one miraculous magic bullet. Instead, it has been the accumulation and staking of many different things I have done over the years. Like I said, I did therapy, I went to workshops and events for personal growth. I have studied and learned a lot about the human condition, about the differences between a man and a woman in terms of behavior, emotions, and biology. I changed my career from business to acting. And acting, though it is not therapy as all my teachers used to say, it has helped me to heal many wounds through the exercises and all the characters I've had to play over the years.

If I had to pick one moment or event that propelled me forward in leaps and bounds was when I realized I had been living most of my life in my masculine energy, even before the abuse. This happened in a Tony Robbins event called *Unleash the Power Within*. The abuse, as I mentioned before, was a magnifier for many issues I had. So, I began to learn and study this subject in depth. I began to transform my life through a deeper spiritual practice (not religious) and through the enhancement and use of my feminine energy. This has allowed myself to enjoy new aspects of life that were unknown or would scare me before. I was able to enjoy my sensuality and my sexuality for the first time. I was able to revive the woman that got buried on that fatal April afternoon. Actually, I have become a much better version of her. I have been able to separate the evil men from the rest and hence, not see them all as one of the same. I have become an avid defender of men, of those decent, good hearted, caring and well-meaning men. I have even been able to thank my attacker, for if it wasn't for him, I probably would not be the woman I am, as I mentioned before, nor would I have created my project called **ACT FEMININE**, in which the vision is, "To create a world where women and men collaborate, cooperate and co-create their shared world together."

And now back to you, Nana. I would like to tell you that if I knew then what I know now, I would say to you "Do not keep the pain inside. Talk to those who love you and share your feelings with them. A huge weight of the pain we carry is released when we share it."

"You will be able to smile and feel true profound joy again. You just have to continue walking through the tunnel, there is beautiful bright light on the other side."

All men are not made equal. Don't lump them all together. Most are good friends, parents, brothers, fathers, and partners. If you heal, they will be able to come into your life to take care of you, love you and protect you as you deserve. Your life will be worth living!

Love you always!

Nana Ponceleon

August 2022.

About the Author

Nana Ponceleon was born in Venezuela. She got a Bachelor's degree in Business Administration with a minor in Computer Science from Pace University in New York. She worked in sales and marketing for companies like Phillip Brothers and Microsoft where she worked for over 12 years, among others. She left the corporate world and decided to make a dramatic change in her career. She moved to New York for the third time in her life, this time to study acting.

Today she is a full-time actress, writer and producer. She has worked in over 30 films, TV shows, many commercials and plays. She has appeared in movies like the Venezuelan film "La Hora Cero" which won many international awards and was featured for over a year in HBO. Last year she performed in an Off-Broadway play at Theatre Row in NYC called "My Mother's Severed Head", where she played the character of "Mother". This play was produced by Bruce Willis and gifted her with two awards, Premio Arte and Premios ATI. She also was nominated for best supporting actress in England's "Rainbow Umbrella Film Festival".

She created a project called ACT FEMININE by Nana. The vision is to "Create a Movement Where Women and Men Collaborate, Cooperate, and Co-Create Their Shared World Together." This project was inspired by her own personal journey and it will soon evolve to include men. She feels there is a huge crisis in the world right now impacting people's lives, relationships, and the planet which can benefit from this vision.

Dearest Maureen,

Writing this letter is difficult. There are so many things I want to say, yet I know I've only learned them with age. I can only hope you read this with an open heart and an open mind, and it solidifies your belief that you truly can change your stars by simply trusting yourself.

Life will not seem fair, and it is through no fault of your own. First, I need you to know that your mom is doing the very best that she can. Although it may not seem that way, she is truly trying to be better than those who came before her. That can feel like a mountain that is simply too high to climb, but please trust me; she is trying to climb higher. Trying to figure out a way all on her own to erase the legacy of a family that has always had the odds stacked against them. You will see a beautiful, strong, confident woman who takes care of everyone, and is the one true constant in the lives of every person in her family. But there are two sides to everyone, and the other side is a frightened, unsure woman carrying the weight of her family's expectations. Never forget that you will always be the most precious gift to her.

The things you will experience that are out of your control do not define you, and will not define you throughout your life if you simply remember there is a lot of life to live beyond the years you spend living in your parent's home. You will feel different; feel as if no one knows or will understand what you have been through. You may feel unworthy of a bigger life. It's simply not true. No one person's life is as perfect as it appears to you, so don't be afraid to simply live the life you hope to live. Work for it; fight for it if you must.

You will feel that going to college will be too hard; that you can't manage it, or won't be able to attain a degree. Do whatever it takes to go! Take a moment to figure out what it is you really want for your life, then get as much education as you can. Having a degree will open doors for you.

SAVE YOUR MONEY! I know it will feel as if you have forever to save, but time passes too quickly. Start small if you must, but make sure you save money each and every payday. PAY YOURSELF FIRST! And, educate yourself on how to best invest your money for it to pay for retirement. It's never too early to plan.

Do not rely on being in love to make your dreams come true. YOU ARE THE FAIRYTALE and are capable of creating a life you love. Be particular about who you invite to share it with you. Trust your instincts when it comes to love. Believe that a man who is willing to build a relationship with you is better than a man who comes along and tells you what you want to hear. If you have to work too hard, and are not laughing often WITH each other, do not be afraid to move on.

Travel. You may fear flying, but push that to the side and just explore!

One day you will be a mother. It will be the most rewarding, but most difficult experience of your life, and you will never know another love like the one you feel for your child. But your childhood memories may try to interfere, cause you to panic and question every decision. Other moms will "suggest" their way of raising their children is best, and you may believe them. Don't. YOU will know your baby better than anyone. And, God will gift you with one who doesn't want to be like every other child. Embrace it! Learn from your child. Listen to what your child needs. You are her perfect parent. Do not doubt what you know about the world around you, and will pass along.

Your life will be a series of very big triumphs, and very harsh falls. You may feel yourself growing tired, questioning even your own existence. It's okay. It just means you are either tired or know you are not where you are supposed to be and afraid to move forward. MOVE FORWARD....IMMEDIATELY. Life is filled with opportunities and possibilities; more than you will ever imagine.

Do not compare yourself to anyone. Do not allow others to tell you who you are. We are all individuals put here to find and nurture our passions and purpose. Do not allow anyone to veer you from the path you choose to walk. It will change, and you will change along the way. But, you will always know what is best for you. Do what is best, even when it hurts.

Never doubt that hope always floats, if you believe you can you will, and NOTHING IS IMPOSSIBLE. You have much to share and teach others. Just step into it, and create the life you love - YOUR LIFE.

Live by these three simple words - ALWAYS BE WILLING.

You are a warrior with a gentle soul.

Trust in you xoxoxo

Maureen Spataro

About the Author

A motivational speaker, and a surthriver of multiple sexual and domestic violence traumas which began at the age of 6, Maureen released her first book "Press Pause; The Breakdown That Rebuilt My Life & Changed a Family Legacy". In addition, Maureen was a contributing writer for Bella Magazine with her column "The Beauty of Giving", and has shared her message of surthrival and hope as a speaker at Georgian Court University in Lakewood, NJ, the Attachment and Trauma Network Conference in Washington DC, The Lightworkers Series at the NJ Arts Center, and What's Your Story USA. As a guest on several podcasts and shows including Sonstein Sundays and Women in the Loop on iHeart Radio, Wheelhouse, B*Inspired, and This Is It TV, Maureen's goal is to share what it took for her to go from "emotional and internal deafness" to creating a life she loves. Recently, Maureen was asked to launch her peer-led support group for The Stephanie Parze Foundation, founded in the memory of Freehold, NJ resident Stephanie Parze who was murdered at the hands of her abusive ex-boyfriend.

"The single most important ingredient to moving past trauma or any adversity we face in life is willingness. When you are in the depths of despair, working through grief, starting over, or trying to move beyond any type of trauma words like strength, courage, resilience and hope are impossible to relate to. The pain you are experiencing blocks your ability to see those traits within yourself; traits that exist in all of us. But, willingness? When someone says they are willing, they are saying "I will try". And, each step taken slowly unlocks the strength, courage, resilience and hope we possess. Our willingness to "put me first", do the work required to release the pain we carry, and clear that space within for all the good that awaits to land is the groundwork we lay in order to build the life we love."

In February 2022, Maureen re-launched Marilyn's Place. Marilyn's Place is a place for women to gather for peer led support, clinician led workshops, one to ones, and social gatherings. Maureen's dream is to open homes throughout the country, and expand the concept of Marilyn's Place to build a community for women to live, rent free, for a year in order to save their money, complete school or and have a fresh start to create a life they love and deserve, in safe and supportive surroundings.

Dear Juliet,

It's 2016

You are living with a man who is miserable and verbally abusive. He constantly reminds you you're not good enough, pretty enough, smart enough, etc. You finally decide to leave him and pack your car with all your belongings. Then you find out you are pregnant. Your family and friends have no idea how much you are suffering because you're too ashamed to tell them the truth about your relationship.

You spend many nights on your own waiting for him to come home or call but he never does. He doesn't answer your calls either. He's out and you have no idea where he is or what he's doing. You know he's lying and cheating, but you have no proof other than the gut-wrenching feeling in the pit of your stomach.

You are terrified of being pregnant and alone, so you stay.

One evening, he comes home after being gone for days and you approach him, asking where he was. He ignores your question. You ask to see his phone and he hands it to you then snatches it back. You attempt to grab the phone and he pushes you to the floor. He doesn't hit you but this is not the first time he has pushed you down. You want to leave him but every time you think you're done, he pulls you back in with his manipulation and lies. He says he is sorry and promises he'll change so you give him another chance.

You're 8 months pregnant now and you're about to walk into an appointment with your midwives to check on your baby when he tells you "You should have had an abortion."

You are devastated. You have spent the last 8 months nurturing a deep connection with the little girl growing inside of you. There were many moments like this leading up to the birth of your daughter.

It's 2017

Your daughter is born.

She is the brightest light, giving you strength, you did not know was in you. Her precious eyes shine as she stares at you, filling you with love. Your devotion as a mother is strong and you do everything in your power to make sure she feels loved and taken care of.

Your partner is still so disconnected and your relationship gets worse as you fight more often than you get along. The energy at home is heavy and you feel like you are raising your daughter alone.

One evening, you're having a conversation with him and he begins to panic as he tries to cover up another lie. This is your breaking point. Your daughter is 6 months old and you have finally found the strength to ask him to leave. Something testing yet empowering happened when you ended this relationship.

The separation forced you to take a long look in the mirror. You suddenly had to face yourself because there was no one there to blame anymore. It was time for you to take responsibility for your life, your choices, and the ways in which you were choosing to show up. You knew in that moment that you could not properly love and nurture your daughter if you did not learn to love and nurture yourself first.

You began to read books, write your own children's book, listen to podcasts, meditate, and focus on things that supported you as a person and a mother. Life still felt extremely difficult as you were raising your daughter mostly on your own. Her father was absent for months at a time because he was angry at you, not understanding the pain he was causing his daughter in the process. He blamed you, saying you destroyed and separated your family. He was angry, spiteful, and manipulative. You did your best to carry on despite his efforts to continue to bring you down.

There were moments where you felt overwhelming guilt for ending the relationship. Whenever these feelings would arise, you would look at your daughter to remind yourself of what you both deserved.

After doing much self-development work on your own, you decided it was time to look for support outside yourself. You signed up for a 3-month self-development workshop. You worked with many coaches as you dug deep, getting to the root of all your self-hatred and insecurities. Soon it became very clear why you attracted that relationship. You didn't love or value yourself. You didn't believe you were worthy of being with someone who treated you with love and respect

Time passed as you immersed yourself in healing and releasing trauma. You became lighter, happier, and more confident. You started to take your goals serious while working towards a better life for yourself and your daughter. You began to fill your cup first so that it would be overflowing for her. Your bond with her blossomed and you grew a mutual love, trust, and respect.

Dear Juliet

It's 2022.

I am so proud of you.

The challenges you overcame were presented to bring you strength, courage, and discipline.

Your ex still blames you and tries his hardest to suck you into his pain and misery. You pray for him and forgive him often.

Your children's book is out in the world, bringing families closer by teaching the importance of hugs.

You are currently hosting workshops to support women in releasing trauma while empowering them to be the greatest versions of themselves. You have accepted that growth is endless and you will be evolving for as long as you are alive. Your challenge now is to learn to be present and aware in the moments where those insecurities creep back in.

As you evolve, you will be tested often and old ways of thinking and acting will come back up. It's up to you to remind yourself of who you are. Confident, loving, patient, and forgiving.

You are in a relationship with a man who supports you, sees you, values you, and treats you with kindness, patience, love, and respect.

You are a warrior, a goddess, and the embodiment of love. You are a warm comforting light for all who get to experience your presence.

Love Always,

Me

About the author

Juliet Meagher is a first-time children's book author. She recently graduated from an emotional intelligence program, which connected her deeply to her purpose. She is a mother of one, yet feels called to love and help children all over the world.

Passionate about being a living example of the change she wants to see in the world, Juliet created, <u>What Is A Hug?</u> To bring families closer together, including her own.

Her intention is to have parents unplug from their own distractions and reconnect, heart-to-heart, with their child – and in their child's world.

Dear Marissa 2010,

Wow, have you been on a journey. It's crazy to think that 12 years ago you felt so broken and lost. Self-Love after enduring all the garbage, and people who abused, ridiculed, lambasted and bullied you felt like an uphill battle. But the outcome was worth the climb. I remember hating you. I remember not being able to look in the mirror because who I saw was a broken, small, worthless person who didn't have value, talent, intelligence or opinions that mattered. I saw a teary-eyed pathetic person that I would constantly criticize, almost mimicking the things that Dave would say to you. And that negative self-talk daily beat down was toxic. I was prolonging my own insecurities, and my own abuse, and I am so sorry. I didn't need Dave anymore; I was doing his job. I gave him rent-free space in my mind to keep you traumatized and feeling worthless. And I just kept finding more guys like him to keep making you feel worse and worse until you felt like nothing. The quality of people that I allowed into your life was horrific. But these creatures were exactly the people you needed to put you on a path to healing. So, for that, I'm not sorry.

I imagine who I'm talking to right now while I'm writing this letter, is you, sitting in Amanda's house on her staircase, writing in your yellow notebook about all the ways he's making you feel, and all the hatred that you have towards yourself and him. Meanwhile, he's at the kitchen table with all of your friends, drinking and having fun, but glaring at you through the railing, and you can feel it. The heat coming from his eyes and pouring into your chest is debilitating. I also know that tonight is the night you take your first steps towards healing. Tonight is the night that you find your voice and stick up for yourself for the first time since the beginning of this relationship. When he tells you he's going out after the party, and you stand your ground, his blatant disrespect for you is the final straw… for now. And even though that's not how it all ends, that taste of freedom and of power feeds your soul enough to know that you do have strength left in you. It's hidden under months of abuse, sexual assaults and gaslighting. But it's not totally dead.

This journey you're on, it's not going to be a cake walk. Getting through the nightmares, the trauma and the poor decisions in relation to who I allowed access to your, body, mind, and spirit, was the most difficult part of the journey. Recognizing the quality of people that you deserve will be trying, but ultimately, you'll get there. You have to learn how to be vulnerable, and with whom it is safe to be that way. There will be days where you feel hopeless, lost, and misunderstood. Those days are limited and temporary. You will have bad days that make you wonder if you're actually crazy and worthless. The vast rewards you'll feel for the misjudgments and mistakes you'll make along the way will be well worth it. It's so weird to be saying this, because obviously it's too late for you to read this letter, but I don't regret anything I did to get me to where I am now. The things you'll do, as irksome as they might be, all created the perfectly imperfect, strong and independent person who is writing this letter today.

You didn't know it yet, but those notebooks you carried, and the things you wrote in them were probably the most valuable resource you could have had. I mean honestly, before you even knew how writing would change your life, you were doing it. And it just felt right. And from those notebooks, and those experiences, your life was reborn.

I remember feeling the power, sitting on Amanda's steps, writing in that yellow notebook. Even though it was one of the darkest days of your life, knowing that Dave was spewing venom at you with his eyes over every word you wrote because he was afraid someone would see it, or because he couldn't control it... I don't know which was worse for him... you knew you had power. Well, not "knew," but felt. If you could have that power over him just by sitting by yourself and writing in a notebook nobody would see for years, somewhere deep down, you knew your life wasn't over. This was not the last of you. You were just too beaten down to see it at the time.

Learning to love yourself, and reframing all the horrible things that were said and stuck inside your head wasn't easy. It took years of self-work, mirror work, reading books, and doing all kinds of exercises to release those words before I could look you in the mirror again and see who you truly are: A strong, brave, courageous badass who has overcome some horrendous obstacles. And baby, that's only a SMALL testament to the strength that you've amassed.

My god! You're leading packs of people who, from all over the world, seek you out to heal with you. Who want to listen to what you have to say. I can't wait until that moment when you finally take a deep breath and feel the wave of refreshing energy filling your soul. That moment was bliss, and 100% worth the struggle.

Things you probably can't even imagine doing, I am accomplishing. And that's because I learned how to love myself again. I learned to trust myself and my judgement, and can rely on my opinions and instinct. Things that Dave thought he took away from you for good, in order to manipulate you and hold you back, I now hold near and dear to my heart.

My best advice to you, beautiful 19-year-old Marissa, is to just keep trying, and love your journey. Don't give up. The biggest steps you took lead to the greatest battles and wins. And though they ended teary-eyed and alone, sometimes eating your body-weight in chocolate and ice cream with

Kristine, they led you here. So, keep pushing. Keep trying new things. Keep yourself open to love. And keep learning and growing. All of these small steps, and all of the little things created a strong, awesome, courageous person who was born to overcome and change the world.

Self-love is a journey. It's about learning to accept your emotions, and put yourself and your well-being first. The more you learn to love yourself, the more incredible decisions you'll make. You're going to set some strong boundaries and not waver, and that's because you learned to have your own back and trust your judgement again. Follow your instincts. You always know the right answer, the problem is whether or not you trust yourself. You should always trust your gut, because it will always have your best interest at heart. Even when you aren't sure, you're filled with self-doubt, or you're haranguing yourself with the same words Dave used to keep you feeling small, you are smart, observant, intelligent, sharp and worthy.

The things you experienced and the ways you felt, feel so foreign to me now. It doesn't feel like they are my memories. It feels like I'm telling someone else's stories. And on one hand, that's a really great thing. It's a much more beautiful and enjoyable life feeling freed from the guilt, shame, trauma and self-hatred that led me to some of the darkest times in my life. But on the other hand, feeling so far removed from the pieces of myself that were shattered by Dave, Iggy and the numerous other abusers and narcissists that broke you, almost makes me feel unreal.

Ultimately though, working through everything, and finding the self-love that you deserve has made the biggest difference in the quality of my life. The people that I allow in my space now is tighter and healthier than ever. The quality of my romantic prospects only got better, until marrying Larry and literally feeling the most emotionally stable I've ever felt.

I'm overwhelmed with the feelings of peace and security, knowing that there is someone in my life who is just as healthy and safe as I am, and as I need him to be.

***"Life is not about waiting for the storm to pass.
It's about learning to dance in the rain."***

Keep dancing, and live that beautiful life that you deserve. Take the good with the bad, and create some awesome stories… I know we will.

Love Always,

Marissa 2022

About the Author

Marissa F. Cohen is the Founder of the Healing From Emotional Abuse Philosophy™, and the Award-Winning and 5-Time Best Selling author, whose titles include: <u>Breaking Through the Silence: The Journey to Surviving Sexual Assault</u> (2018 Readers Favorite International Book Award Winner, and #1 Amazon International Best Seller); <u>Breaking Through the Silence: #Me(n)Too</u> (Amazon #1 Best Seller), <u>The Ruhe Approach: Healing From Abuse</u>, <u>The Healing From Emotional Abuse Philosophy: The 3 Keys to Overcoming Narcissism,</u> and <u>The 5-Must Know Tips for Nurses: To Feel Prepared and Confident When Working with Domestic Violence Victims</u>. She has been recognized as an expert, thought leader and change agent by Jack Canfield, James Malinchak, Brian Tracy, Kevin Harrington and Joe Theismann.

As the Founder of the Healing From Emotional Abuse Philosophy™, she has created a 3 Key Method to overcoming narcissism and narcissistic abuse. Over 3,000 people have used this Philosophy to start living free, confident and peaceful lives through her one-on-one coaching programs.

Marissa F. Cohen was named a Top 10 Most Inspirational Female Entrepreneur on International Women's Day 2021, and has shared a stage with Jack Canfield, Patty Aubery, Joe Theismann, and James Malinchak.

Marissa's Podcast, Healing From Emotional Abuse, has charted in the Top 10% of all podcasts globally, ranking as high as Top 5 in Albania, Top 10 in Hungary, Top 20 in New Zealand and Italy, and Top 100 in Australia, Israel, Egypt, Canada, Malaysia, Norway, Russia, and South Africa. Top 200 in Denmark, Sweden, Germany, Great Britain, She is also the host of a weekly radio show on KXFM Laguna Beach that reaches over 24,000 listeners.

As a speaker, she has trained demographics across the board from practicing nurses and nursing students, to first responders, to students across the country, and military leadership about how to effectively respond to sexual assault and domestic violence survivors. And has trained over 5,000 college students about healthy relationships and how to be a good friend and partner. The things that are crucial to socialization that are not taught in schools.

Her mission is to educate students about healthy and toxic relationships, enabling them to make informed and educated decisions, and recognize red flags immediately. She wants to see all survivors of sexual abuse, narcissism, emotional abuse and domestic violence release their trauma, build resilience and rebuild their lives, so they can feel complete, happy, and confident.

MARISSA FAYE COHEN

Do you have a story that you want to share of overcoming your personal traumas and finding self-love again?

The *Love Yourself First Series* is looking to connect with people who desire to share their stories and inspire others to find self-love, healing and growth. If you have dreamed of impacting people with your story, and helping others to learn and grow from your personal experiences, we want to hear from you.

If you dreamed of bringing your messages of hope and love to a larger audience, then this is for you.

If you dreamed of inspiring others to share their stories and see that they're not alone, then this is definitely for you!

If the letters in this book have inspired you to write your own letter, and you want to share that journey with us, send your letter to:

Me@MarissaFayeCohen.com